NELLIE BLY

DIANE GEOGHEGAN
MARY WILLS
602-634-0255

MAIN STREET
P.O. BOX 758
JEROME, ARIZONA
86331

KALEIDOSCOPE RENAISSANCE

By

COZY BAKER

Van Dyke, Ltd., Series II

Beechcliff Books

Printed in the United States of America
by Hagerstown Bookbinding and Printing

Library of Congress Catalog number 92-073477
ISBN: 0-9608930-4-0

Photographs by:

Laurie Bridgeforth: pages 66, 67 lower, 117 lower, 119, 120
Kinsell Coulson: pages 13, 31
Mary Alice Dwyer: page 107
George Erml: page 114 lower left
Peter C. Fellows: page 113
Jill Fineberg: page 55
Paul Larsen: page 153
Lisa Masson: title page, 8, 17, 20 & 21 lower, 24, 26 top, 28, 65,
    69, 70 top, 71, 115, 116, 154, 155, 157 (scope), 159 middle, 180
Olan Mills: page 77
Steven Minkowski: page 179
Adam Peiperl: pages 3, 4, 16, 33, 39, 43, 53, 156 top left,
    156 lower right, 160, 172, 173
Vincent J. Ricardel: page 108
Wayne Source: page 178 (hand and ampules)
Swanson Images: page 107
Cover of "Martyr of Science," reproduced and used as back-
    ground for text, with the permission of the Royal Society of
    Edinburgh and the Royal Scottish Museum, page 9.

All illustrations: designed and executed by Jan Haber
Design layout: Perk Hull

Beechcliff Books
100 Severn Ave., Suite 605
Annapolis, MD 21403
(301) 365-1855

Kaleidoscope Renaissance
is an updated, revised, and amplified version of
Through the Kaleidoscope... And Beyond
and *Kaleidorama* by Cozy Baker.

It is dedicated to my precious grandsons
Kevin Michael Baker
and
Davis Oliver Richardson
May they, along with you, dear reader,
discover within the kaleidoscope
magical fantasy, wonder, and moments of splendor!

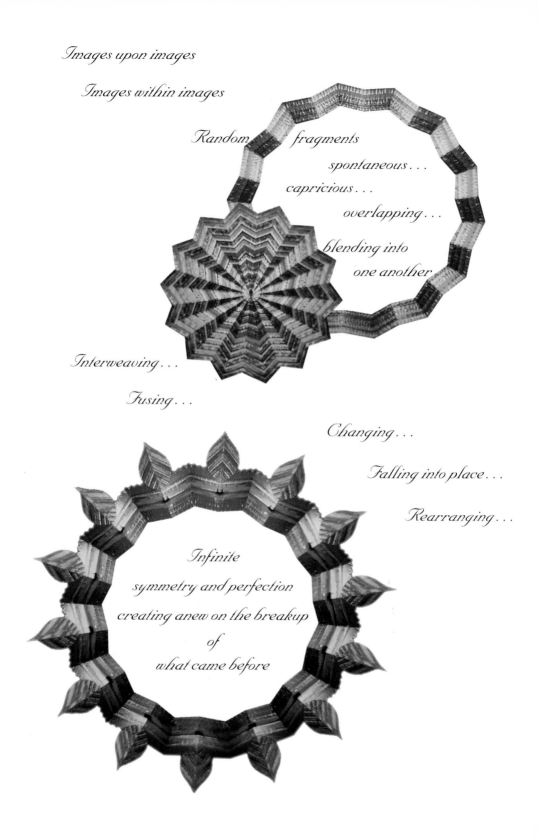

Images upon images

Images within images

Random   fragments

spontaneous...

capricious...

overlapping...

blending into

one another

Interweaving...

Fusing...

Changing...

Falling into place...

Rearranging...

Infinite

symmetry and perfection

creating anew on the breakup

of

what came before

The Kaleidoscope lets your spirit soar
and your heart dance.
It endures because beauty, magic, and wonder are timeless.

Commemorative poster of the first Kaleidoscope exhibition.

Kaleidoscope. The very word promises the magic of Cinderella's coach and Aladdin's lamp. Dancing colors conjure up childhood fantasies. Popsicle pinks, lollipop purples, Cracker Jack gold, and iridescent bubbles all burst forth with the excitement of Fourth of July fireworks.

Yes, kaleidoscopes captivate everyone. A person's age, race, sex, or skill does not seem to matter, but rather the possession of a sense of wonder and a delight in beauty.

CONTENTS

Once Upon a Scope

Original books by Brewster, vase by Jerry Hovanec with silver inlay of a Brewster scope, 19th century extension prism, early kaleidoscope teaching tool, Spectroscopes by Browning and a Brander concave mirror, circa 1785, with its original box.

The Inventor

Sir David Brewster

1781 — 1868

*I*mages and colors have been reflected since water appeared on our planet, and objects have been multiplied since the advent of mirrors. But not until 1816 was this magic phenomenon put together in one optical instrument. Sir David Brewster took the first giant step in the creation of the kaleidoscope.

David Brewster was born in an obscure country town in the midst of the Scottish lowlands on December 11, 1781. He was somewhat of a child prodigy. While yet only ten years old, he constructed a telescope, significant of the chief bent of his work and genius. Nature endowed him with some of its choice gifts: close observation, unceasing inquiry, and a scientific proclivity. Far before his peers, he absorbed all that was available in elementary Scottish education. Because he evidenced exceptional aptitude for learning, his family decreed that he should study for the ministry of the Church of Scotland. Thus at the tender age of twelve, he was consigned to the University of Edinburgh, where he continued his intellectual achievements. Indeed, he was greatly admired at the University for his unusual academic ability and was generously welcomed into the intimate fellowship of the then-distinguished professors of philosophy and mathematics. To cap off his "formal" education, at age 19 an honorary Master of Arts degree was conferred upon him. This carried with it a license to preach the gospel as a minister of the Scottish Established Church.

Of his brief pulpit episode, James Hogg, a colleague, wrote in a letter to Publisher James Fraser:

"... he was licensed, but the first day he mounted the pulpit was the last — for he had then, if he has not still, a nervous something about him that made him swither when he heard his own voice and saw a congregation eyeing him; so he sticked his discourse, and vowed never to try that job again. It was a pity for Kirk [the National Church of Scotland],... but it was good day for Science. ...for if the doctor had gotten a manse, he might most likely have taken to his toddy like other folk."

This was in the year 1801. He immediately turned his great talents to the study of optics, and for twelve years conducted a series of experiments which were revealed to the public in "A Treatise Upon New Philosophical Instruments," published in 1813.

Brewster's treatise did not represent his only accomplishments during this period. In 1807, at the age of 26, the University of Aberdeen awarded him a Doctor of Letters degree, the highest literary distinction of that era, a truly unique achievement for one of his age. But this was not all; in 1808, he was elected a Fellow of the Royal Society of Edinburgh and the same year became editor of the Edinburgh Encyclopedia, a position he executed with excellence for more than 20 years.

In 1810 Brewster married Juliet McPherson, but scarcely anything is recorded of his family life. Shortly after his death, his daughter, Mrs. Margaret Gordon, about whom little is known, published a biography entitled "The Home Life of Sir David Brewster." But reviewers determined that Mrs. Gordon's work contained more sentiment than analysis or fact and it was not considered authoritative.

It was in the year 1811, while writing an article on "Burning Instruments," that Brewster was led to investigate a theory of Buffon, which was to construct a lens of great diameter out of one piece of glass by cutting out the central parts in successive ridges like stair steps. Brewster did not consider Buffon's proposal practicable. However, it sparked an idea which produced awesome scientific results. Thus was born an apparatus of then unequaled power — the construction of a lens by building it upon several circular segments. Here was a useful invention, later perfected, which produced the lighthouse as we know it, creating light-stabs of brilliance that pierced far into the night to guide mariners.

This breakthrough was followed by yet other honors. Brewster was admitted to the Royal Society of London and was later awarded the Rumford gold and silver medal for his theory on the polarization of light, which states that light reflected from a glass surface is completely polarized when the reflected and refracted rays are perpendicular to one another. Success followed success; and in 1816, the Institute of France adjudged him 3,000 francs — half the prizes — for the two most important scientific discoveries to have been made in the two previous years.

Then, as an added jewel to his already glittering optics crown, Brewster invented the kaleidoscope! This was the year 1816. Brewster was 35 years of age, and was already an established philosopher, writer, scientist, and inventor.

Brewster's kaleidoscope created unprecedented clamor. In a history of Brewster's Kaleidoscope, found in the June 1818 volume of Blackwood's Magazine, Dr. Roget said:

"In the memory of man, no invention, and no work, whether addressed to the imagination or to the understanding, ever produced such an effect. A universal ma-

Photograph of Sir David Brewster by Lord Kinnaird (from a collection of negatives, many taken personally by Brewster), courtesy of Cheryl Gable; Brewster telescopic kaleidoscope with extra cells, circa 1816.

Brewster's door (right of bicycle) with commemorative plaque, St. Leonards, St. Andrews. The Brewster family lived here for 23 years while Sir David was principal of combined colleges of St. Salvator and St. Leonards.

Gravestone of Brewster, his wife Juliet, and their two sons James and Charles

nia for the instrument seized all classes, from the lowest to the highest, from the most ignorant to the most learned, and every person not only felt, but expressed the feeling that a new pleasure had been added to their existence."

But while Brewster was granted a patent, was acknowledged and acclaimed for his invention, he did not realize any monetary remuneration. Others did, however. There was some fault with the patent registration and before Brewster could claim any financial rewards, kaleidoscopes were quickly manufactured by aggressive entrepreneurs who sold hundreds of thousands with great financial success for themselves. Like so many other great men, this was to be the pattern of Brewster's life; great intellectual achievement without worldly compensation.

In 1823, the Institute of France elected Brewster a corresponding member. The Royal Academies of Russia, Prussia, Sweden, and Denmark conferred upon him the highest distinctions accorded a foreigner. These high honors opened lines of communication for him with the great minds of Europe.

In midlife, in 1832, he was knighted by William IV. This brought an instant social status that only those few touched by the king could know. But Brewster simply continued to pursue his investigations and experiments. In short, he remained the poorly paid teacher, the famous professor whom James Hogg, in the same letter pictured thusly:

"He has indeed some minor specialties about him. For example, he holds that soda water is wholesomer drink than bottled beer, objects to a body's putting a nipper of spirits in their tea, and maintains that you ought to shave every morning, and wash your feet every night — but who would wish to be severe on the eccentricities of genius?"

One of Brewster's most illustrious moments came in 1849. He was nominated as one of a panel of eight foreign associate nominees of the National Institute of France. So great were Brewster's achievements in comparison to all others that after examination, the institute struck the names of all other candidates and Sir David Brewster stood in splendid isolation as the sole remaining candidate. His discoveries of the physical laws of metallic reflection and light absorption, of the optical properties of crystals and the law of the angle of polarization, along with his improvement of the stereoscope and lighthouse apparatus, surpassed most scientific achievements of that era.

It is for this man's contributions to philosophy and science that he is mainly remembered, but it was by his pen that he earned his living. In addition to editing the Edinburgh Encyclopedia from 1808 to 1830, he was one of the leading contributors to the 7th and 8th editions of the Encyclopedia Britannica, joint editor (1819-1824) of the Edinburgh Philosophic Journal, and then (1824-1832) editor of the Edinburgh Journal of Science. Among his most noteworthy separate publications should be mentioned his *"Life of Sir Isaac Newton,"* *"Letters to Sir Walter Scott on Natural Magic,"* and the *"Martyrs of Science."*

His lifelong love of nature's beauty, his abiding Christian faith and his ability to translate what he had learned into the written word in a way which could be understood even by children earned him the affection and respect of not only his associates and the populace of his time, but also of the generations which followed.

Many facets of Brewster's varied interests were uncovered during research for a symposium held at the Royal Scottish Museum in Edinburgh on November 21, 1981 to celebrate the bicentenary of Brewster's birth. This provided an appropriate occasion to re-examine Brewster's contributions to science as well as to the social and cultural history of the nation. Each segment of his diverse career was covered by an expert authority. Proceedings of the complete symposium were published, including an extensive bibliography of over 200 of Brewster's articles and photos of his optical inventions. (Martyr of Science: Sir David Brewster 1781-1868, Royal Scottish Museum Studies, 1984.)

Paul Baxter, Senior Scientific Officer at the British Library, tells us, for example, that Brewster had an enormous enthusi-

Images
through
Bush scope

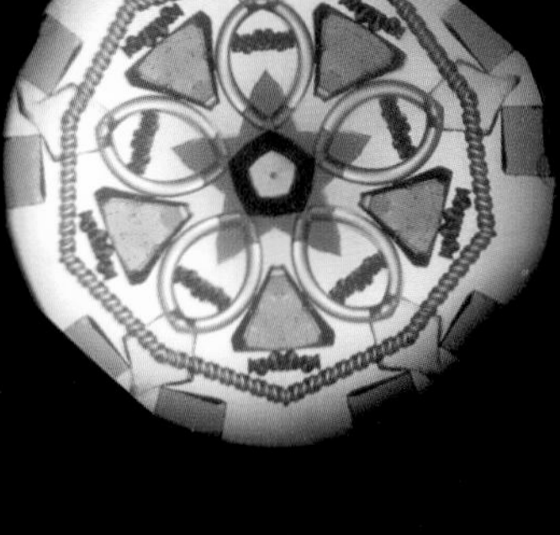

Images through
Original Brewster scope,
R. B. Bate model

asm for a belief in the so-called plurality of worlds, the notion that other worlds were inhabited. John Christie, Lecturer at the University of Leeds, explains that Brewster is one of the very small number of past scientists who wrote history of science which is still consulted and used as history of science by historians of science. "He exists, that is, as both subject and colleague, and that is a rare thing."

Allison Morrison-Low, Assistant Keeper, Dept. of Technology at the Royal Scottish Museum, covers his optical inventions, including the Lenticular Stereoscope, and his interest and involvement with photography and the nature of light.

An album of almost 200 photographs assembled by Sir David Brewster between 1839 and 1850, at the dawn of photography, was published by the J. Paul Getty Museum in 1990. Captions accompanying these pictures, along with the introduction and footnotes by Graham Smith, give further insight into the life and times of our esteemed scientist.

And from Kinsell Coulson's unpublished manuscript of a detailed biography of Sir David Brewster's life we learn that a few months before his 75th birthday, Brewster married his second wife, Jane Purnell, who "in addition to being a most attached companion, gave birth to a daughter who became the bright light in Brewster's declining years."

$\mathscr{A}$MERICA'S $\mathscr{E}$ARLIEST $\mathscr{P}$RODUCER —
$\mathscr{C}$harles $\mathscr{G}$. $\mathscr{B}$ush

Very little is known about the earliest kaleidoscope developments on this side of the Atlantic. Although as early as 1818, a few Americans began experimenting with kaleidoscopes, only one remains of any permanent significance — that of Charles G. Bush (1825-1900).

Bush is somewhat of an enigma. Untrained in any of the physical sciences, he arrived in Plymouth, Massachusetts, in 1847 from Culberg, Prussia, where he was born in 1825. He had worked in his father's kemp manufacturing business and proceeded to establish a successful rope business in Plymouth. In later years, after moving to Boston, he pursued interests in microscopes, telescopes, astronomy, and photography, at all of which he excelled. It was in the early 1870s that he began developing kaleidoscopes.

Bush manufactured his parlor kaleidoscopes by the thousands and they were recognized as extraordinary even then. These instruments had a barrel of banded black cardboard with a spoked brass wheel rotating an object cell, mounted on a turned wooden stand.

Most noteworthy about the Bush kaleidoscopes were the glass pieces contained in the object case. Bush had a basic mix of about 35 pieces, a third of which were liquid filled. Inside the liquids were air bubbles that continued to move even after the object case was at rest. Both the solid and

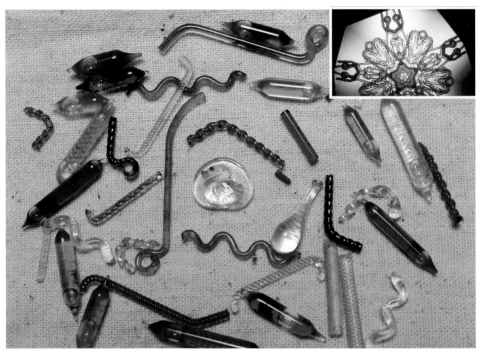

Liquid-filled ampules by Charles G. Bush

*Two Bush scopes —
example of each
stand for which he
was granted a patent*

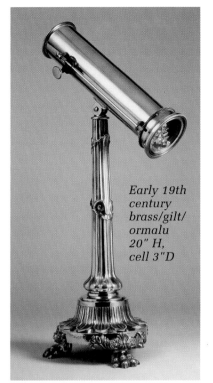

Early 19th century brass/gilt/ormalu 20" H, cell 3"D

From the Cozy Baker collection

From the collection of the late Craig Musser

Early 19th century scopes: English brass scope in orginal box with extra object cells, Sheffield silver scope, rare red morocco leather scope with horn trim

liquid-filled glass pieces were of brilliant and well-chosen colors, and the patterns they formed were the finest of any 19th century kaleidoscope. One unusual piece that comes into view in a very few of the original Bush scopes is a clear glass disk embossed with a swan.

W. Leigh Newton

Bush secured several patents in 1873 and 1874; the first for a new and useful object for the object box — hermetically sealed liquid-filled ampules; the second for a means to add and subtract pieces from the object case without having to disassemble it; one for the use of a color wheel as a backdrop for the images; and another for a four-legged wooden stand that could be disassembled for easier carrying and shipping.

It is hard to believe that this handsome instrument originally sold for a mere $2.00. Today, if one can be found, it might go for as high as $2,000. But kaleidoscope price history was really made at Sotheby's auction in London, March, 1987, when a "good W. Leigh Newton Kaleidoscope, English, circa 1830" went for £17,500 or roughly $32,000. The previous auction record bid for a kaleidoscope had been $5,000, set by the late Craig Musser almost ten years earlier.

Martin Roenigk, a U.S. dealer in antique kaleidoscopes, crossed the ocean to join the bidders. He readily admits it was the most fabulous kaleidoscope he had ever seen, definitely the pinnacle of any collection, and declares that the photograph doesn't do it justice.

But in the annals of kaleidoscope history and to the serious collectors, the R. B. Bate Brewster Patent Brass Kaleidoscope, English, circa 1820, is still regarded as the most important antique kaleidoscope. This polyangular instrument is distinguished by both its unusual conical shape and the ability to change the angle of the two metallic mirrors simply by twisting the body of the scope. The barrel and stand are made entirely of brass and the construction is of the finest museum quality.

Only nine of the 90 thought to have been made are accounted for — four in museums in London and Scotland, one formerly in a museum but returned to its owner, and four in collections in the United States.

Steven Manufacturing Company

It was during the Victorian era that the kaleidoscope reached its zenith. Then as the age of electronics advanced, the popularity of the kaleidoscope as entertainment for the family waned. Though they did continue to find their special place in Christmas stockings, kaleidoscopes remained for the most part on the shelves of toy and novelty stores. And the company most responsible for bridging the early rush of popularity and the current renaissance was Steven Manufacturing Company.

Steven's toy business was started in 1946 by Roscoe Zimelman. Roscoe's little son, Steven, saw a kaleidoscope at a friend's house and wanted it. When his dad couldn't find one in a store, he made one, then another, and another. And that's how Steven toys began.

Approximately 15 different models were designed and manufactured by the Steven Company, including designs for Campbell Soups, Corning Glass, Pepsi, and the Mickey Mouse scope for Disney. To date, the Steven Company produces in excess of 400,000 fine toy kaleidoscopes each year for children of the world to enjoy. The popular model #150 with a turnable object case can be found with many colorful graphic changes over the years.

In 1960 Mr. Bev Taylor, a former magician who had joined the Steven Company, bought the toy firm from Roscoe Zimelman's widow. He kept the Steven Manufacturing name

19th century English and American kaleidoscopes

From a collection of antique and old toy scopes

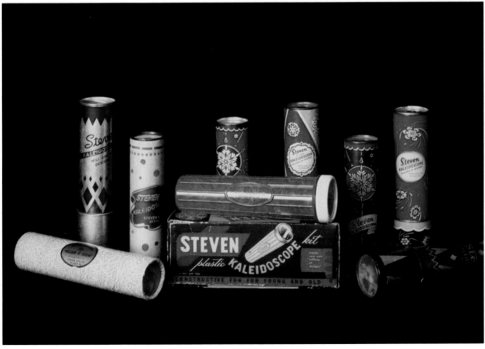

Early scopes from the Steven Manufacturing Company

and continues to manufacture good-quality, colorful, inexpensive toy scopes.

Lew Sprague, a collector and researcher of old scopes, insists that, "A kaleidoscope collection would be incomplete without an example of at least one "American made" Steven toy kaleidoscope."

Trovascope

Another pre-renaissance scope, made of cardboard and lacking first surface mirrors, that has both classic and historic significance is the Trovascope. Many current collectors started with Ernest Trova's Falling Man Kaleidoscope, produced by the Museum of Modern Art in New York in the early 70s. Taking a recognizable form (his "Falling Man"), Trova uses positive and negative space and through the magic of mirrors allows us to concentrate our attention on small segments at a time, repeated into a new pattern. He also includes a few other common objects to add color and movement.

From Brewster to Bush to Baker
(history in the making)

Since its invention in 1816, the kaleidoscope has fulfilled a variety of functions, serving as a toy for children, a center of parlor entertainment for adults, and a design palette for all those in the ornamental arts who use beautiful forms and patterns.

During the past decade there has been a dynamic renewal of interest in kaleidoscopes. Allowing the eye to marvel, the mind to explore, and the soul to soar, these mirrored tubes of magic are being recognized and accepted as an important new art form as well as a positive therapeutic and inspirational influence.

Spawned in the '70s, and continuing into the '90s, this unprecedented kaleidoscope renaissance essentially evolved during the 1980s. An article in the November 1982 issue of Smithsonian Magazine helped spark the kaleidoscope revival. Jeanne McDermott's words and Wayne Source's photographs titillated the curiosity of some, nudged the nostalgia in others, and started this author on a spirited quest. Only seven artists were mentioned in the Smithsonian article: Steven Auger, Carolyn Bennett, Peach Reynolds, Dorothy Marshall, Bill O'Connor, and the late Craig Musser and Judith Karelitz. Other serious artists, however, were creating and marketing their scopes during this same period and many, many more swiftly followed.

The year 1985 heralded the publication of the first book to be written on the subject of kaleidoscopes since Brewster's Treatise on his invention in 1816: "Through the Kaleidoscope," by Cozy Baker. At the same time, Cozy curated the world's first major kaleidoscope exhibition at Strathmore Hall Arts Center in Bethesda, Maryland. Designers, collectors and lovers of scopes from coast to coast came together in the suburbs of Washington, D.C., for a glorious celebration of color, cre-

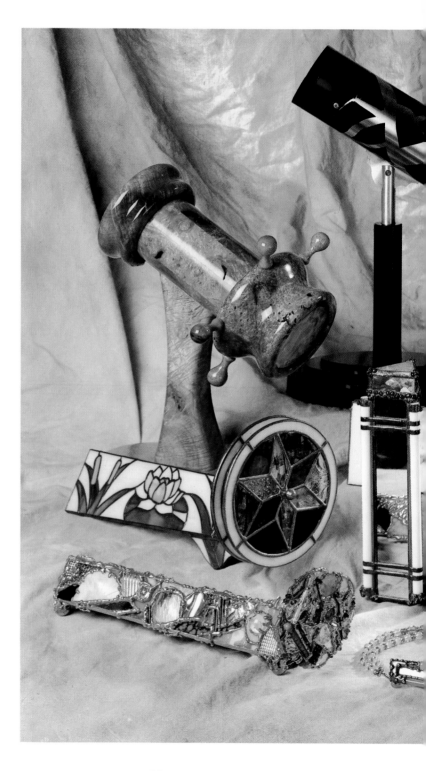

Contemporary scopes (clockwise from left front):
Gallocolley Glass (also necklace),
David York, Randy Knapp, Spirit Scopes,
Ray Howlett, J & J Beall, Sheryl Koch,
Shantidevi, Mike Gallick, Kaimana Art Glass,
(center): Ann and Pete Roberts, Kay Winkler

ativity and design. During the month-long show more than 10,000 visitors viewed kaleidoscopes designed by nearly 40 contemporary artists.

Local and national media gave kaleidoscopes added visibility with print, radio and television coverage. *The New York Times, USA Today, The Washington Post* and *The Baltimore Sun* were among the nation's first newspapers to chronicle this renaissance. The glowing accounts in these leading publications were followed by a host of others: a spot on The Voice of America, National Public Radio, and NBC's Nightly News; articles in *Scientific American, Victorian Homes, Sky, Antiques & Fine Arts, Collector Editions, Southern Accents, Traditional Homes, Modern Maturity, U.S. Air, Diversions,* and *Forbes.* Kaleidoscopes were rapidly becoming the rage.

In the spring of 1986, Cozy created and organized the Brewster Society to provide a communication network between artists, designers, retailers, collectors, and lovers of kaleidoscopes. This international organization continues to publish a quarterly newsletter to keep enthusiasts up-to-date on who's who and what's what in the world of kaleidoscopes as well as where to locate kaleidoscopes, exhibitions, and Brewster Society meetings. An annual convention enables people of kindred spirit to meet, share ideas and view new kaleidoscopes.

In September 1986, a second exhibition was presented at Strathmore Hall Arts Center. Three dozen new artists were added to the roster of kaleidoscope exhibitors.

In 1987, a revised edition of *Through the Kaleidoscope* was published. *Through the Kaleidoscope...And Beyond* updated the progress and expansion of kaleidoscopes which had occurred since publication of the first book.

In 1988, the Smithsonian Institution Traveling Exhibition Service sponsored a three-year exhibition. With emphasis on the scientific more than the artistic, *Kaleidoscopes: Reflections of Science and Art,* designed by Dorothy Marshall, traveled to 18 cities in the United States and Canada.

In April 1989, the first Brewster Society Convention was held in Louisville, Kentucky, in conjunction with the Fourth Annual Kaleidoscope Show at the Kentucky Center for the Arts. Members from 29 states gathered for a brilliant kaleidoscope jubilee. Then, in September, Strathmore Hall Arts Center presented "Kaleidoscopes '89." During the four-year interval since the first exhibition in 1985, the number of artists had grown from under 50 to nearly 100.

Each year increasing numbers of people discover kaleidoscopes and the joys of either collecting or making them.

The current renaissance embraces an enthusiasm for the increasing variety of new innovative creations and an appreciation for the rare antique instruments. Kaleidoscopes of every vintage are becoming the most captivating collectibles in the country.

Cozy with statue of Sir David Brewster
at the University of Edinburgh

"Tea with Auntie Twila"
(the Symmetroscope, circa 1899)

Portrait by Barbara Mitchell

Modern Kaleidoscopes
Structure, Styles, and Mirror Systems

Its colors are the sparks from rainbows

Dancing, darting with endless surprise

Its patterns are the wings of angels

Unveiling wonders in mirrored disguise

Structure, Styles, and Mirror Systems

Today's kaleidoscopes are extraordinary. Produced by hand in America, they are the finest in the world. Combining 19th century tradition with 20th century talent and techniques, they reflect the past as they mirror the future. Although new styles and inventive variations are continually being developed, basically, all kaleidoscopes are a variation of one simple equation:

1 eyepiece + 2 or 3 mirrors x an object = beautiful image

The shape of the image is determined by the number of mirrors and the angle at which they are placed. The color and pattern are determined by the objects to be viewed.

Ordinary mirrors are not suitable for a quality scope as they do not provide clear, sharp reflections. First- or front- surface mirrors that have a reflective coating on their front surface are essential for first-rate viewing. Light reflects only once from such a mirror, which gives a sharper image. Regular mirrors are coated on the rear surface, so that light is reflected twice, leaving the edges of the images fuzzy.

There are two major *types* of scopes:

Kaleidoscopes — with moving colors at the object end.

Teleidoscopes — using only a clear lens at the end, which turns whatever it is pointed toward into a kaleidoscopic image.

The two main *styles* are hand-held and pedestal or parlor.

The items to be viewed fall into two major categories:

Object cell, case, box, or chamber
- filled with tumbling items
- liquid-filled with floating items
- empty, to allow personal choice and change of items
- polarized-light material and filters

Objects themselves
- wheels or disks, fixed or hollow
- marbles and hollow spheres
- turntables or carousels, attached or separate
- tubes

EVERY KALEIDOSCOPE IS BASICALLY A TUNNEL OF MIRRORS

The number of mirrors and their angles will determine what you see

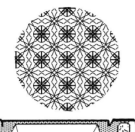

A kaleidoscope with 3 mirrors will produce an entire field of patterns.

A kaleidoscope with 2 mirrors will produce a single circular design.

SCOPES WITH DIFFERENT OBJECT ENDS PRODUCE DIFFERENT VIEWS

CHAMBER SCOPES have an enclosed object case filled with jewels, flame sculptured glass, beads or other objects, such as seashells. The contents tumble freely.

FLUID CHAMBER SCOPES have an object case filled with fluid (usually oil or glycerine) and assorted jewels, flame sculptured glass, beads or other objects, such as seashells, which drift through the fluid.

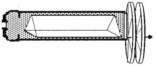

WHEEL SCOPES have one or more wheels which turn to change the view. The wheels may be of hand painted, leaded or fused glass, slices of semi-precious stone, pressed flowers or combinations of these.

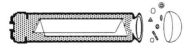

INTERCHANGEABLE 'SCOPE features a removable object end. You can remove the objects inside and put in your own.

TELEIDOSCOPES owe their magic to mirrors and lenses alone: there are no moving parts. Whatever you point it at will appear multiplied. A teleidoscope transforms the whole world into a riot of kaleidoscopic images.

Diagram: Shel Haber

Most object cells have clear glass on the side facing the mirrors and translucent glass on the other side. Some are made of plastic. A new type of object cell has a black backdrop and is side-lit.

The baubles and trinkets inside the object cells are limited only by the imagination. Along with shards of flame-worked glass, beads and gemstones, there can be dried flowers, feathers, buttons, shells — and on and on. The more varied in size, shape and texture they are, the more intricate the image, and the more beautiful the objects, the lovelier the image.

Just as each note is essential to a complete symphony, each piece in the object cell is equally important to the whole design. Curlicue and labyrinthine imagery in some reflects the romance of yesteryear, while flashing L.E.D.s and fibre optics in others foretell a hi-tech, computerized tomorrow.

The body of the scope is generally structured in the classic geometric shapes: cylinder, triangle, square, and rectangle. Some, however, assume the shape of particular things such as airplanes, trains, buildings, lighthouses, hot air balloons, fruit, a gavel, or the ever-popular egg.

From simple toys to space-age spectaculars, kaleidoscope exteriors vary almost as much as the changing patterns. Wood and stained glass are the materials most frequently used. Every type and hue of exotic wood is employed, from the creamiest bird's eye maple to the richest purple heart and bloodwood. And the scopes of glass run the gamut: stained glass, blown glass, painted glass, slumped, fused and sagged glass, beveled glass, pyrex glass, dichroic glass and glass rods. Other materials utilized for the body of the scope are brass, acrylic, ceramic, copper, Corian, mirror, anodized aluminum, fabric, leather, bronze, alabaster, and paper. A few kaleidoscopes are even crafted from such unlikely items as sea shells and birds' eggs.

There are scopes one can wear, smell, listen to, and feel. Sizes vary from miniature to man-size. Prices vary from under $5 to over $5,000. There are simple cardboard tubes with metallic mirrors containing plastic bits and pieces. And there are scopes made of sterling silver and 14-karat gold with rubies and emeralds.

Other variations include binocular scopes for both eyes, projection scopes for screens, and there are scopes that are motorized, sound or touch activated, and gear driven. Some contain their own light source, a few incorporate more than one type of mirror system, and others are polyangular (in which the angle of the mirrors changes). There is one that uses an air-filled bellows to blow the pieces about, the wheels of yet another are rotated by pressing keys, and one is built into a wooden cane.

As the demand for customized scopes increases, the innovations keep pace. Kaleidoscopes are being installed in ceilings and skylights of homes, built around fish tanks and water fountains, constructed into silos, and formed from balloons.

Mirror Arrangements

There are two major systems of mirrors in kaleidoscopes: the two-mirror, which produces one central image or one cluster of images, and the three-mirror, which produces innumerable images throughout the entire field of view. Both are set up in a triangular configuration — in a tube similar to a prism.

In the two-mirror system, the mirrors are arranged in a "V" with a third side that is blackened. The angle of the "V" determines the number of reflections. Alda Siegan explains the effects of the two-mirror arrangement as "somewhat similar to standing in front of a dressing mirror having a side leaf mirror. The closer the angularity between the mirrors, the more reflected images of your face."

The most perfect symmetry and best images occur when the angle between the mirrors divides equally into 360 degrees.

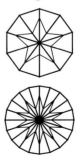

60°	— 6-fold symmetry	— 3 point star
45°	— 8-fold symmetry	— 4 point star
36°	— 10-fold symmetry	— 5 point star
30°	— 12-fold symmetry	— 6 point star
22.5°	— 16-fold symmetry	— 8 point star
20°	— 18-fold symmetry	— 9 point star
18°	— 20-fold symmetry	— 10 point star
15°	— 24-fold symmetry	— 12 point star

Three-mirror   *Two-mirror*   *Four-mirror*

The three-mirror system can be arranged in any form of triangle, so long as the sum of the three angles equals 180 degrees. It produces a continuous field of honeycomb-like patterns.

The 60°-60°-60° equilateral triangle is the most common and produces the least attractive pattern. The 90°-45°-45° gives a more interesting symmetry. But the most enjoyable image produced by the three-mirror system is the 30°-60°-90°, which contains three types of symmetry: fourfold (from the 90° angle), sixfold (from the 60° angle), and 12-fold (from the 30° angle).

Other systems, such as square four-mirror configurations, produce repeated square patterns, while four-mirror rectangular configurations produce repeated rectangular patterns. The images created are striped patterns, since the reflections move directionally up, down, right, and left.

Cylindrical tubes lined with a reflective material will produce a spiralling effect. Since there are no angles involved in this style, the reflection seems to climb through the tube asymmetrically.

Tapered mirror systems provide a spherical 3-D image when viewed through the larger opening.

The polyangular arrangement is the most elaborate and satisfying. It is a variation of the two-mirror design in which one of the mirrors can be adjusted, changing the angle of the "V" and thus the number of reflections. It is possible, therefore, to produce a wide range of symmetrical patterns.

It is also possible to build two or more separate mirror systems into the body of a scope, each with its own eyepiece and viewpoint of the object.

MODERN KALEIDOSCOPES
Facets and Fascinations

The kaleidoscope speaks silently
Whispering secrets to man's inner space
Colors infuse the spirit with rapture
As interlaced patterns dance into place

Facets and Fascinations

Kaleidoscopes have recaptured the heart and imagination of America. Appealing to each gender and every age group, they provide the nostalgically familiar coupled with a hint of surprise.

But what is the kaleidoscope's impelling fascination? What makes people so effusive? In other words, what is the real secret of their appeal and why do people collect them?

Collector Pat Seaman answers, "There is something magical about kaleidoscopes. I don't understand it. I just accept it."

Kathy Arnold, collector and shop owner, quickly responds, "You make it come alive." Then, after a little thought, she adds, "Yes, it is the participatory element that appeals to me — you can hold it, make it move or take it with you. You just look at paintings, for instance, but with kaleidoscopes, you are in control because you can change the image."

Ray Donarski, another collector, laughingly exclaims, "Oh, it's a terminal disease."

Several couples use their scopes as an intercom; leaving messages for one another in the form of an especially beautiful image to be shared.

While the nonverbal communication of kaleidoscopes may transcend words, just introduce two collectors and the communication becomes quite vocal. Sharing and swapping scoops on scopes is almost as exhilarating for a scope-lover as unearthing an old Bush or discovering a good source for new kaleidoscopes.

One collector expresses it this way: "I head for them whenever I feel depressed — and it isn't only looking into them, it's just knowing they are there like friends. When I was a child, books were my friends. They were sold and I miss them. Now, kaleidoscopes help recapture my favorite moments of childhood."

Another collector says, "Kaleidoscopes are like classical music — something you can enjoy and revel in all by yourself."

An interior decorator replies, "Kaleidoscopes create a magic atmosphere. Artistic in design and eclectic by nature, they are a perfect decorating medium."

Yoga teacher Peggy Rude gives her answer: "Besides the beauty, I think there are many lessons we can learn from the kaleidoscope, one of the lessons being, to let go of concern for what has been and enjoy the beauty and blessings that exist right now."

Linda Shellenberger, co-owner of the Nestegg in Bar Harbor, Maine, was perhaps that rare child who never had a kaleidoscope. Her ongoing fascination didn't begin until 1987, but it involves "anticipation of discovery...beauty waiting to be glimpsed, like the light at the end of the tunnel. I think of the kaleidoscope," Linda continues, "as a private showing of fine art in a constantly evolving gallery."

Joel Lerner, a business professor, suggests, "Kaleidoscopes now may also have the ability to grow in value and to turn a wonderful hobby into a financial investment."

Bruce Haney, on the other hand, an investment counselor in Omaha, Nebraska, advises, "Instead of thinking about the kaleidoscope's future appreciation, just appreciate its daily dividends of beauty and joy."

But for those who might collect with an eye to investing, art conservator Judith Paul points out several factors to consider:

1. quality of workmanship
2. pieces that are signed and dated along with any supporting documents
3. importance and reputation of the artist (is he an innovator or a replicator?)
4. is it a one-of-a-kind, prototype or limited edition?
5. aesthetic merit (very personal)
6. has it received any awards, honors, or been published?

For the most part, designers, collectors and retailers alike seem to agree that kaleidoscopes miraculously combine the frivolity and merriment of fairyland with the innermost strata of the spirit. They make faraway dream time not so far away.

Cynthia Donahue certainly captures this sentiment in her poetic response:

In each kaleidoscope there is a world — waiting to be discovered,
then visited — at any time — at one's own choosing.
There lies within, a peaceful silence, of beauty and loveliness.

Deep in my grown-up being, the child feelings stir,
remembering how it was to get down really close
to the earth — look, ever so carefully
through green blades of grass–down where
other small beings made pathways
along the crystal grains of sand – where one
would wait, breathlessly, quietly, to catch
a fleeting glimpse of those that lived there -
those fairies' wings – those mystical caves;
or to remember the magic in a crystal dewdrop
where, if one looked closely, one could see
the whole world – reflected – even oneself
or the world in a clear ocean pool
where one could gaze intently – down to the
very bottom, through the water, to see all
the little creatures living there –
mermaids and seahorses.

Then – there is the other world - the world
of never-ever ending space – the world of
silver stars, the Milky Way, the planets and the moon;
the world of sunlight, and clouds, and rainbows, where
my childhood dreams came true and I could soar
and glide and whish and zoom and feel the
closeness of angels – up there – in the clear
blue darkness of the sky.

There are so many worlds to find,
so many dreams to dream.
These magical, mystical moments are there for me -
in my kaleidoscopes.
All I have to do is look, into that wee small opening,
that viewing place – and rejoice that my paradises,
my tearful ecstasies are not lost.

Meditative and Therapeutic Values

As each mandala unravels, another unfolds

Rearranged . . . realigned . . . renewed.

Patterns resolve in mosaics of perfection

Mysteriously merging into symbols of wholeness.

Meditative and Therapeutic Values

The kaleidoscope renaissance is more than a revival of interest in scopes and goes beyond a prolific array of intriguing optical instruments. Bringing together in one object cell a unity of light, color, form, and motion that seems to capture moments of eternity, the kaleidoscope "inspires the mind" and "calls the heart." It is one form of art that is continuously being created right before the viewer's eyes. The static has been removed and the imagery lives, equating itself to life's experiences.

Mandala

The kaleidoscope image takes on meaningful significance when it is associated with the age-old mandala. Mandala, quite simply, is a circular symbol of wholeness. It is a circle expanding from its individual center as it interrelates with other circles, radiating from their center, all being one with the creative universal source. It is a circle whose center is everywhere and whose bounds are nonexistent.

Jose and Miriam Arguelles have written in their book, "Mandala," Shambala Publications:

"The Mandala is the symbol of the round of life and death, of the cosmic procession of beings, planets and stars, of earthly seasons and galactic cycles.

"The integration of worship, knowledge, and beauty is a significant feature of the Mandala, enabling it to convey a teaching to the receptive. The Mandala expresses a knowledge of the laws of harmony. It is not concerned with the personal but with the transpersonal; not with the fugitive and the arbitrary but with the eternal."

There are three basic elements inherent in both the mandala and the kaleidoscope: a center, cardinal points, and symmetry. In a mandala, as in the patterns of a kaleidoscope, a succession of interlinkings are unified into one whole. Each piece is a vital part of that whole, no matter how small. Take one piece away and the image is not quite the same.

Beyond its inherent beauty and captivating magic, the kaleidoscope symbolizes life — a mandala in action. Man is the center. The awakening of intelligence is the first radiating circle, spiraling from the center and proceeding from there, each person's mandala is as individual and distinctively different as a fingerprint.

The unfolding drama of human events and emotions tumbles and spills from an inexhaustible source on no apparent course. But the universe is fashioned and governed according to a principle of divine order. We sense it, we know it's there, but the breadth and complexity of its patterns make it invisible to our mind's eye.

Only man's awareness and attunement to the Creative Original Force determine whether the patterns in his mandala fall at random or seek a meaningful direction. The archetype referred to by Carl Jung represents a pattern of order in which each content falls into its proper place and the tumbling pieces are held together by a protective circle — the microcosmic enclosed within the macrocosmic.

Meditation

For some, the kaleidoscope is a "happening" — a joyous experience — a celebration of color. For others, it is a meditative device, a lens opening onto an inspirational stratum of rarefied light.

Even Webster, with his vast comprehension, did not fully fathom the myriad facets of the kaleidoscope. So, I have coined a new word — mediscope: to meditate as you look through a kaleidoscope, and breathe the colors, while listening to inspirational music.

Meditation is a natural process, and we discover it at some stage of the soul's development. It is for the purpose of realizing, attuning, and centering with the Supreme Life Force.

Color meditation is not new, but the mode of procedure has always entailed mentally recalling a color and then concentrating on it. How much easier and more efficient to visually observe color while looking into a kaleidoscope. The kaleidoscope's images represent possibilities, opportunities and new horizons created from random disorder, chaos and shattered dreams. The kaleidoscope is also a great emotion-stabilizer. It is virtually impossible to hold a grudge, harbor resentment or feel any negativity while enjoying the visual experience found within its perimeter.

To observe and breathe color takes neither physical effort nor mental gymnastics. Simply slow down the rush of thoughts and enter into stillness. Let the mind as well as the eye absorb the regenerating energy from each color that comes into view. Open the windows of your inner space, allowing the light to focus on every feeling, emotion, and creative idea. Breathing deeply, retreat into the center of your being, letting color engulf you. Continue to inhale the very essence of the colors that please you most or make you the happiest. Feeling rather than reasoning, wait until there is an intuitive knowing that all the pieces are falling into place, until you sense a oneness with the universe and a unity with mankind.

The following is a meditative affirmation by psychotherapist Jeanie Robertson of Atlanta, Georgia:

Intrascope Affirmation

I am a source of light. I strive to radiate and reflect the beauty and wonder that is within and around me to others.

My body is the presentation of the light. I do those things which enable me to be consistent and in harmony with the light within. I eliminate that which builds conflict and discord. I am a mirror of the light — I determine the balance and symmetry of all dreams, ideas, people, and things with which I come in contact. I strive to provide clarity and quality within my being. I am a true reflection of the light.

I am a chamber for the light. I collect within my being those objects which provide the color, texture and variety of that which is really me. I examine my memories, relationships, plans and fantasies to insure the best and most honest representation of myself. I build on those qualities which create harmony with the light source. I break down into components that I can handle, all that blocks me from the light.

I am the eyepiece of the light. I provide the window through which the patterned beauty of the spirit can be seen. I am willing to take risks, to be vulnerable, to demonstrate that which I am continually constructing and reconstructing in the light. Being connected with the power, I am a light source.

Metaphor

Life unfolds from the center
New beginnings emerge from the breakup of past forms
All things turn and spin and change
Endlessly rearranging themselves
The world is truly a kaleidoscope

The kaleidoscope is equated as a metaphor to many conditions and realities: change, order evolving from chaos, and the process of creation itself. The following lines are by Linda Joy Montgomery, a poet and photographer who lost her sight. She refers to her life as a "Kaleidoscope" in a poem by that name:

...My life is a kaleidoscope
Of changing thoughts and patterns
Evolving into a multifaceted perspective.
Then the colored glass
Becomes precious gems of joy, and truth,
Harmony and balance,
Rearranging themselves
So I can stretch and expand and reach for the Light.

Kaleidoscope artist Dean Kent sees the multifaceted mural of the world as a kaleidoscope. The following is an excerpt from his article, *"A Synthesis of Science and Art":*

"The kaleidoscope can best be understood as a metaphor for a new world perspective. It is as if you took the dizzying multiplicity of people, places, and things in the world and placed them in an object case. Where there was division, difference, and apparent chaos, there emerges integration, similarity, and an organic unfolding.

"The metaphor offers a realization of a connect-

ing, purposeful spirit that envelops the whole earth, connecting all organisms in an endless chain of life. The simple pleasure of viewing a kaleidoscope reminds us of the interdependence and interrelatedness of life on earth. The earth as seen from space is a living mandala, an organic whole, and as an image, forms a foundation for a widening of the human perceptual horizon and a broadening of thought and understanding."

> *"The world is your kaleidoscope,*
> *and the varying combinations of colors*
> *which it presents to you*
> *at every succeeding moment*
> *are the exquisitely adjusted images*
> *of your ever moving thoughts."*
> James Allen

The following excerpts are from an article by Hospice Nurse Coordinator Joyce Lowder, RN, MSW:

From Lessons to Therapeutic Metaphor

Metaphors become therapeutic when they bring about perceptual and behavioral changes. There is something incredibly wonderful about how kaleidoscopes help revive a sense of wonder in terminally ill patients. All human beings have a sense of wonder, but sometimes it gets lost as one moves from perceptions about childhood to those of adulthood and as life becomes more difficult and painful.

When we look into a kaleidoscope, there is somehow a response of body, mind, and spirit. We see with our eyes the color and pattern, think with our brain about how we are seeing what we are seeing, and feel with our heart that there is more to the image (and experience) than meets the eye.

In discussing with the patients how life's experiences are like a kaleidoscope, we emphasize the variety of changes that occur; how they are altered by the color and the light as perceived by the viewer,

48

and we point out that when life looks gray, you can bring color into the picture. Sometimes one picture must be turned loose so another one can appear, and often, the second one is more beautiful than the first.

There is a lot of choice in seeing life with many colors. Explaining the colors as associated with emotions is helpful to some, for example, red relating to anger, blue to depression, yellow to hope, green to life, etc.

Growth and beauty are also used as examples of the metaphor. We talk about how the human being is wonderfully made, how the physical, emotional, and spiritual components are synchronized, but in terminal illness, the physical body deteriorates. The emotions then have to work with trying to balance the decline in physical status and so the spiritual growth often takes on a greater importance. There are times when we talk about the dying person's view of his life and how God, as the ultimate kaleidoscope viewer, may perceive beauty in the way the patient and the hospice volunteers utilize their time, talents and energies.

Therapy

Healthy emotions are as important as a healthy body — perhaps even more so. The kaleidoscope's ability to soothe and stimulate at the same time makes it a perfect balancer. Dr. Clifford Kuhn, a psychiatrist in the Department of Psychiatry and Behavioral Sciences at the University of Kentucky, loves kaleidoscopes. He did not know when he started collecting them that they were an appropriate tool for his profession. He writes:

The essence of health is wholeness, an integration of body, mind, and spirit in equilibrium. Medical research has revealed that many of our current illnesses are the result of the effect of stress which seems ubiquitous in our modern society. Stress is destructive to our body, disorganizing to our mind, and disabling to our spirit. It has been demonstrated that a regular habit of quietly drawing aside from one's usual responsibilities for reflection and relaxation significantly repairs or prevents the potentially destructive effects of daily stress.

Kaleidoscope viewing is one such activity of repair. It is restorative to the body in that it requires physical stillness and stimulates pleasant visual sensations. At the same time it has a beneficial effect on the mind by presenting an endless variety of form and color combinations that stir the imagination and stimulate the intellect. Kaleidoscopes are, likewise, good medicine to the spirit as they reflect the constant emergence of order out of disorder and provide a sense of participation in the creative process. In this way, regular viewing of kaleidoscopes can be a significant contributor to a person's overall health.

A video tape of Barbara Mitchell's SpectraSphere, produced by Pat Kehs of Prime Lens Productions, has taken kaleidoscopic imagery to a new therapeutic level. Many doctors and health care professionals agree that this tape ("A Video of Kaleidoscopic Magic and Enlightenment") is an effective antidote to tension and stress.

It is being used in some hospital waiting rooms and closed-circuit television systems as well as in an increasing number of cancer clinics and hospices. One hospice nurse says, "It can help individuals who are experiencing physical, emotional or spiritual crisis to transcend pain, even if just for a little while."

Whole Brain Corporation

Ned Herrmann, artist, sculptor and founding president of the Whole Brain Corp., finds kaleidoscopes a wonderful tool in determining right or left brain dominance. The mission of the Whole Brain Corp. is to apply new understandings of the brain to the human development needs of individuals and corporations throughout the world.

"To us, the turning of a kaleidoscope symbolizes the rearranging of stored information to constantly create new patterns — new approaches to problem solving; different colors change patterns of feelings."

Teaching people how to see things and change their patterns of thinking is part of the work accomplished at Ned's Applied Creative Thinking Workshops in Lake Lure, N.C., as well as those offered in public facilities around the world. During more than 100 of these workshops, Herrmann determined that creativity "is a definable and teachable process that can be learned and applied.

"For many of our participants, the kaleidoscope is an effective way of expanding their visual processing capability," Herrmann reasons, "stimulating their imagination, and in the process, helping to break down the walls that have accumulated since childhood. After working with tens of thousands of individuals over the past decade, I am convinced that for many people the acquisition and application of creativity is more the breaking down of walls than the building of skills. I have long held the view that creativity is natural and normal in children and begins to be less available as

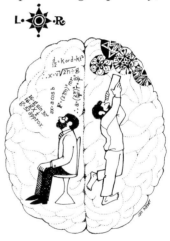

children mature and experience life's situations. The simple re-experiencing of some of our childlike wonders can reawaken those delightful childhood experiences that we had with our first kaleidoscope.

"I am particularly impressed with the Illusion kaleidoscopes by WildeWood Creative Products, based on Cozy Baker's idea of combining a space tube with a teleidoscope. I use the Illusion as an illustration of the difference between "creativity" and "innovation." In terms of new ideas, they represent two paths to success. I think of the act of creating the kaleidoscope originally as pure *creativity* in the applied sense. I think of the space tube in a similar way, as being *creative* in its own right.

When we combine them as was done with the Illusion kaleidoscope, we are *innovating* around two existing original creative concepts. One of the reasons behind the success of the Illusion is that the combination of *two creative ideas* makes it extremely powerful as a visual experience.

"Since dominance is acquired more by nurture than by nature, it is quite possible to change a person's brain dominance profile through education, skill training and life experiences. If a left-brained person wants to stimulate the right side, he might develop an interest in kaleidoscopes."

The following description of the right brain explains why "kaleidopeople" have a right-hemisphere dominance.

"The right brain is our visual brain. It is where we recognize faces as contrasted to names, and it is where we do our nonverbal thinking. For most of us, it is the center of intuitive and insightful thinking, where we can process information simultaneously and where conceptual thinking can take place. It is the location of our ability to synthesize as opposed to analyze, and this is where we can deal with holistic concepts, that is, where we can see the forest as opposed to the trees. Other parts of the right hemisphere are specialized in the areas of interpersonal processing, emotional thinking, and music appreciation."

This is the day-dreamer's corner, the area that allows the thinker to "see the big picture" — read signs of coming change, invent innovative solutions to problems and recognize new possibilities. Right brainers observe from a whole point of view, seeing the end at the beginning, and they need a lot of space.

Contemporary Designers

With varied patterns

   new perspectives evolve

With each color

   diverse feelings emerge

Continuous change

   stimulates imagination and creativity

CONTEMPORARY DESIGNERS

The artist is as important to many collectors as the kaleidoscope itself. Each artist strives to infix into his work something intrinsically and distinctly his own. Kaleidoscope connoisseurs are often able to identify a kaleidoscope without seeing the artist's signature.

There are many good kaleidoscopists who are not included in this book. This in no way diminishes their work. I have written about the ones who have initiated some original or unusual element in their scopes and become part of the kaleidoscope community by participating in the exhibitions and events which have ushered in the Kaleidoscope Renaissance.

Each designer named on the following pages is a true kaleidoscope artist. That means he or she creates scopes from his or her own ideas and imagination. Not content to duplicate existing work or rest on the laurels of their reputations, the designers continually refine, hone, and improve their work. Sophisticated design, intricate mirror arrangements, precision tooling, and professional workmanship distinguish these artists as today's outstanding exponents of excellence. Dr. Brewster would be proud and, no doubt, amazed.

B. T. Ansley, IV

B. T. Ansley, IV is one of the newest kaleidoscopists mentioned in this text. He is also using a material new to the kaleidoscope industry—alabaster. Ben has incorporated this idea in the copyrighted design of his one-of-a-kind kaleidoscopes. The subtle diffusion of the light by the alabaster creates an almost magical environment for viewing the Venetian millefiori he uses as the color objective.

When the library at Yale University was built, the scholars and engineers wanted the most perfect light possible for viewing and reading. They decided on translucent alabaster windows, since the light passing through them was as close as they could come to perfection.

Ben has been an artist since childhood. For 25 years he pursued a business career while at the same time serving as artist in residence at Cameron University in Lawton, Oklahoma. Ben is also an ex-regular army officer, paratrooper, private pilot, gourmet cook and collector of fine wines.

Ben confides, "It was the beauty of the people making kaleidoscopes as much as the beauty of the scopes themselves that really inspired me to get back into the art world."

Stephen Auger

"I have always viewed working with reflective symmetry as a sacred discipline," Stephen Auger states. "To me it is a gift of the physical universe, to see into her workings. In my paintings I work with primary color energies, creating color harmonies. Kaleidoscope harmonies resonate within the heart and spirit."

As an artist, Stephen Auger was creating paintings which explored the harmonic relationship between light and color long before he discovered Brewster's formula and designs for kaleidoscopes.

Always a plodder, Stephen pounded the pavements of New York City, hauling his portfolio, trying to get introduced to people who could appreciate his work. To make ends meet, he painted fabrics for fashion designers. It was while he was so occupied that he met Gene Moore, the man who had been designing Tiffany's windows for thirty years. Moore permitted Auger to place five paintings in Tiffany's windows and he sold them all.

Scopes proved a natural for Stephen, whose other interests include physics and optics. Combining his artist's eye for color and form with a scientist's passion for precision, Stephen developed a very special series of kaleidoscopes.

"The Auger Collection" is a one-of-a-kind, acid-etched solid brass kaleidoscope made in four sizes, with each one signed, dated, and numbered. Semiprecious stones and liquefied glass drawn into spirals, loops, and whimsical shapes form the basis for the gorgeous visions — a full orchestra of color in a capsule.

When I read the brochure describing Stephen's new "Parlor Kaleidoscope," I phoned immediately to order one, sight unseen. When it was delivered I was delighted beyond telling. It was all that the brochure promised. I don't believe his words can be improved upon:

> *"Exquisitely realized and beautifully crafted, this American Parlor Kaleidoscope quietly explodes in an intense orchestration of images. Brilliant colors are brought together in stellar patterns of infinite intricate complexity. The rotating object case holds sparkling treasures, delicately shaped glass and semiprecious crystals. Each piece is carefully chosen and collected to produce harmonic cadences of color. The resultant, radiant play is endlessly changing and utterly seductive in the magic of its vivid timbre.*
>
> *Equally beautiful is the object itself. Precision-machined and painstakingly assembled by hand, this kaleidoscope will be treasured for generations. It is adjustable and of solid brass on a walnut base with each surface polished and detailed, and each material glowing in its own patina. Measuring twelve inches high and twelve inches long, this American Parlor Kaleidoscope has an authoritative presence equal to the splendor that its images convey."*

On the *"American Parlor Kaleidoscope (Series I and II),"* Stephen collaborated with Tom Raredon, a designer trained and excelling in metallurgy.

In Auger's two necklace kaleidoscopes, one sterling and one champlevé, the optics are composed of a crystal prism (instead of mirrors) which has been ground with razor-sharp edges. Because of this unique optical system and precision workmanship, the scope will remain dust-free and crystal-clear forever. Each piece is one-of-a-kind. From start to finish, Stephen Auger is working to create state-of-the-art optical instruments that are truly "jewelry for the mind."

Don Ballwey

The Tutankhamen Exhibition inspired Don Ballwey to craft some kaleidoscopes that would live beyond his existence here on earth. He carved a mold out of graphite for hand pressing glass scarabs and other treasures for his scopes, and this emulates the quality of longevity which he admires in Egyptian work.

The fact that the black fertile soil surrounding the Nile was an integral part of Egyptian life prompted Don to use black iridescent glass, along with the vibrant blues and purples associated with their royalty.

Don admits to becoming absorbed in fantasies while he is creating, which involve a great king who is interested in looking for exciting works of art by a local artist. "One of my goals," Don explains, "is not only to have the present owners enjoy my work, but also to have their great, great, great, great grandchildren get the same enjoyment."

Audrey Barna

Audrey Barna is first and foremost an eggist. When she was searching for a type of egg art that no one else had ever done, she got the idea to make one of her goose eggs into a kaleidoscope. It struck the fancy of the scope community and Audrey conducted a class at a Brewster convention where many of the scope artists tried their hand at making an egg scope.

Today there are several people making scopes in real eggs and others using the shape of the egg. But, for the record, Audrey Barna made the first goose egg scope and has continued to make a few. (page 155) Most of them are beaded and no two are alike, making each of them a one-of-a-kind. Audrey finds that "They are therapeutic to make and an outlet for creativity."

Carolyn Bennett

By studying *"How a Young Lad Can Make a Kaleidoscope From A Tin,"* in an old "Book of Knowledge," a young lassie was launched on her scope-making career. Most children are intrigued with kaleidoscopes at one time or another, but then they are tossed aside for a new diversion. Carolyn Bennett never lost the initial fascination.

She remembers, at age eight, visiting the Corning Glass factory, where in a choice between two souvenirs, she passed up a kaleidoscope in favor of a trinket. She kept wishing she had opted for the kaleidoscope. Needless to say, the story has a happy ending.

Even while Carolyn was teaching art, she always kept on the look out for tubes — recycling any she could find into scopes. The more she made, the more she wanted to make. Finally, Carolyn resigned her teaching position to do what she loved most — making kaleidoscopes. "I like to think of scope-making as a perfect combination of many art forms," Carolyn says. "When I mix pieces of glass inside a scope, it is like painting. When I design the exterior, it is sculpture." She hand paints some of her scopes and coordinates the colors inside. In others she floats sea shells in a clear liquid. And new waters were charted when Carolyn introduced the kaleidoscope as wearable art in the form of a necklace.

Acrylic is the material Carolyn prefers to work with, finding it sturdily transparent, without being fragile. But it is the crystal quality permitting illusion beyond illusion that captures her imagination.

Starting with small, simple hand-held scopes, Carolyn Bennett has graduated to large sophisticated pedestal models. In addition to the first modern acrylic parlour scope, "Odylic I," Carolyn soon presented "Luna"– a scope as seductive as the glow from the moon! Luna has a sleek black anodized aluminum body with polished silver rings. By unscrewing one of the rings, object chambers can be changed. Each "Luna" comes boxed with a stand to hold the scope and its extra chamber. Additional chambers can be purchased or custom chambers can be made with one's own treasures. Its narrow-angle three-mirror system produces an intricate image that glows against the dark background with an amazing radiance.

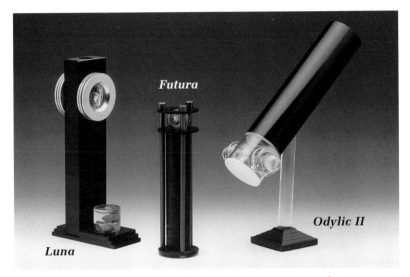

Futura

Odylic II

Luna

Customized and personalized scopes are popular items at C. Bennett Scopes. Counted among its commissions are large industrial organizations, children's museums, and amusement parks. Once there was a request for one with a very special message. Looking inside this surprise scope, the recipient read the words, "Will you marry me?" Evidently the results were positive, because more message scopes have been added to the line.

Versatility and variety are definitely a scopemark of C. Bennett Scopes. From tiny "little jewels" that can be worn around the neck, to six-foot outdoor scopes, and from romantic hearts and flowers to streamlined high-tech, C. Bennett Scopes offers more than thirty models.

Carolyn's prolific output is equalled only by her positive outlook. "There is a very mystical and personal experience happening when a person looks through a kaleidoscope," she observes. "Although I place the colors in the chamber, it is the viewer who controls the scope with his own karma. He steps into his own private world of vision and only he sees, feels, and understands that moment. I feel blessed that I have been able to share with people something beautiful that may be inspirational to them."

Henry Bergeson

Henry Bergeson has taken old forms and found new ways to create self-contained pieces of art. Light sources from within and without, changing images drifting through the lenses and the sensual pleasure of well-polished wood are the definitive characteristics of his work.

Images of change also characterize Bergeson's life and his evolution into an imaginative, innovative kaleidoscope maker. Once a New Englander who learned the painstaking craft of woodworking helping his father refurbish old boats and old buildings, Bergeson now lives in the foothills of the Colorado Rockies.

Studying and working on old boats dominated his early years. Then, with his father, Bergeson began sailing from Norway to Maine in a 1905, 42-foot yawl, *Cockatoo,* in 1979. But the voyage ended disastrously about 600 miles south of Iceland when the *Cockatoo* was mortally damaged in heavy seas. The two were rescued, and the boat was left to drift off into the fog. The danger of the experience seems to have provoked a change in Bergeson's approach to life, stripping away the conventional as unimportant.

After graduating from college, he became a mechanical engineer and helped design modern sailing rigs for cargo ships.

But as the *Cockatoo* had been cast adrift, so too was Bergeson. The more immediate, hands-on work of the individual, not the requirements of corporate life, became his focus.

Corda Lee

He set out for Colorado without knowing how his "land voyage" would end. He met a stove and clock maker, borrowed equipment, and translated his first ideas about kaleidoscopes into the "treasure chests," which allow viewers to mix and mingle small objects into ever-changing patterns of light and color.

He continues to refine and redefine his work. The mountains have become his home, but small objects such as sea shells still float in his kaleidoscopic imagery. "I like my own environment for sure," says Bergeson. "I like to make things, and I like to make nice things." And he does!

Mary Boll

As a collector, Mary Boll was disappointed not to find a scope that incorporated fiber-art textures, so in 1990 she designed her own woven-wheel kaleidoscopes. They are made in three different sizes with individual weavings done on a four-harness hand loom. Two stained glass wheels form the viewing patterns. One wheel has a small woven tapestry that matches the weaving in the body of the scope. Decorative solder is used where the wheel rod attaches to the scope base.

Mary also makes candle scopes which were inspired by the following excerpt from Brewster's Treatise on the Kaleidoscope: "In these experiments, the reflecting plates were necessarily inclined to each other, during the operation of placing their surfaces in parallel planes; and I was therefore led to remark the circular arrangement of the images of a candle round a centre..."

"Brewster's Fire" is a large stained glass scope 18" tall, 19" long, and 6" wide, with two image trays which accommodate four candles. The inner candle holder is attached to a music box which turns mechanically. The outside candle tray is moved manually so that the viewer can control the image.

"Barbara's Gift" is a smaller version with only one tray holding one candle. While it is made in a variety of colors, a white one, with a red candle placed in a flat green wreath, makes a splendid Christmas scope.

Alfred Brickel

The Guinness Book of World Records does not have a category — yet — for kaleidoscopes, but Alfred Brickel did receive a letter from Guinness Superlatives, Ltd., stating that his was the largest on record.

The World's Largest Kaleidoscope™ weighs 500 lbs. and is 12 ft. long and 6 ft. high. The object box is 48" in diameter and the viewing image is 36". The box is 23" x 10-1/2" x 77" and it is operated with gears and pulleys.

Al Brickel is president of KaleidoArt, a division of Newe Daisterre Glas®, an art glass studio which does handcrafted custom work. The World's Largest Kaleidoscope™ was made to order for a bar in Cleveland, which never opened. Al is happy that the scope not only survived, but is appreciated even more today.

Its operation is totally different since the 4' object box, which he refers to as a "squirrel cage," rotates on a horizontal plane. It is made for comfortable viewing while standing and the image changes by the turning of two ship's wheels. Almost any type objects can be easily inserted, providing multiple effects — a kaleidoscopic merry-go-round.

Rather than break his own record by building larger and larger ones, Al makes half-scale and quarter-scale models of the world's largest.

Peggy Burnside
Steve Kittelson

To make the unique round glass barrels used by Woodland Glass, Peggy Burnside and Steve Kittelson developed a special mold to "drape" or "slump" the glass over in an electric glass-firing kiln at a temperature in excess of 1200° F. After many hours of annealing and cooling, the two halves are ground to fit together. They then apply a patina to the solder, buff, and protectively coat the solder with lacquer. Some of their barrels incorporate cut pieces or blown glass shards that form designs which are fused flat before bending.

Each object cell contains pieces of glass which they make either by flame-working with a high temperature torch or in a glass-blowing furnace. A vast palette of colors and dichroic glass affords them a range of tones seldom seen in scopes, giving the viewer jewel-like images of exceptional quality.

They construct each object cell, and it is only after the desired balance of hues is achieved that the individual cells are filled with glycerin and sealed.

Peggy and Steve are attuned to the song birds and wildlife in a secluded valley in northeast Iowa and feel that "Kaleidoscope images are very much like moments in time that we must enjoy fully because once they are gone, we can never duplicate them. They are also like human beings — they come in a wide variety of exteriors, but one must look inside to see the true beauty unfold."

Dale Bush
Jim Koscheski

Dale Bush and Jim Koscheski (Big Muddy Woodworks) make a fine line of affordable handsome wood teleidoscopes. They are well-crafted and come in several sizes, with slightly varying shapes. A few combine dual exotic woods, such as cocobola and ebony. A few kaleidoscopes are also made at Big Muddy Woodworks, but the main emphasis is on teleidoscopes. Dale says, "They present a different view of the world - and it is often an improvement."

Shorty Chase

Marion Cornet Crouze Chase, best known as "Shorty" (6'), was the first to follow the directions for the "Fireburst" that Cozy Baker "unveiled" in the Spring, 1988 Brewster News Scope. (This is the idea that led to the Illusion Scope by WildeWood Creative Products.)

In response to everyone's initial exclamation when first peering into the scope, Shorty named it, "Oh Wow!" Her scopes are known not only for their exciting, dynamic images,

(continued on page 73)

Climbing the stairs:

Four antique scopes
Danny Wilson, Tim Enos
Ron Kuhns
David Collier, Ralph Olson
Van Dyke, Ltd., one-of-a-kind
Van Cort's "Dragonfly"
Brodel and Rosenfeldt
Christie Moody, WildeWood's "Illusion"

Images through Van Dyke, Series II
    by Barbi Richardson

Image through Magna Sphere by Sam Douglas

Clockwise from right rear: Nityaprema, Carolyn Bennett, Don Ballwey, Stan Griffith, Peter and Skeeter DeMattia, (three), Nityaprema, Allen and Michele Crandell, Carmen Colley, Stan Griffith, and clock by Steve Failows.

Images by
Sherry Moser:
left, Chandala
below, Spheara

Clockwise from left: egg by Barbara
Mitchell, Peggy Burnside and Steve
Kittelson, Sherry Moser, Kay Winkler,
Barbara Mitchell, Sherry Moser, (two),
John Culver, Sherry Moser

Bob McWilliam

Lesley Wadsworth

Stephen Auger

Sue Ross

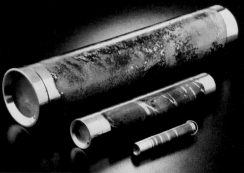

Stephen Auger

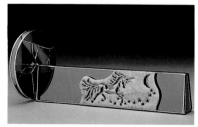

James Dama Hill

Marti Freund

68

Clockwise from back: Tom and Carol Paretti, Steven Gray, Earl McNeil, Ron Kuhn, Randy Knapp

Clockwise from left: J & J Beall, Jon Metzger, Dorothea Marshall, Glenn and Ben Straub, David Kalish, Glenn and Ben Straub

Left to right, front; Dennis and Diane Falconer, Christie Moody,
Back; Spirit Scopes, Charles Karadimos, Sherry Moser

"Let the Dreamers Wake the Nation" Shantidevi and Sugito

Castle and extra wheels by Anneliese Redmond
Interior "Star-Eight" image by Gordon Redmond
(each turret contains different mirror system)

*Images through the scopes
of Chesnik–Koch*

Kaleidoscopes by Janice Chesnik and Sheryl Koch

but also for their unique mirror configurations. While each scope follows the basic design, each is really quite different.

Shorty continues to make a few one-of-a-kind models for some of the larger kaleido-shops, but only when she can take time away from her greatest passion — golf!

Janice Chesnik
Sheryl Koch

Appearing on the kaleid-horizon earlier than most, with perhaps the largest offering of two-wheel glass and brass scopes, is the mother-daughter team known as Chesnik-Koch, Ltd. Actually, the team is comprised of four players, because each of the husbands plays an active role in this kaleidoscope enclave. "When we say 'Kaleidoscopes by Chesnik-Koch,' we mean all four of us," says Janice Chesnik, who was the first in the family to adopt the scope as a way of living.

Janice has been toying with colors since her first crayons. The simple kaleidoscope she owned as a child added impetus to her hobby and her interest in color design. Years later, while attending the University of Kansas, she took a few art courses which gave vent to her creativity through a variety of handcrafts. A move to California, marriage, two daughters and many crafts later, Janice found her true niche, when she incorporated her stained-glass knowledge and experience into the stained-glass kaleidoscope.

Janice was enthralled to be able to create colors and patterns that moved and changed, while at the same time finding a way to turn her leisure-time activity into a profit-making business at home.

When the orders started rolling in and her confidence grew, Janice shared her enthusiasm and know-how with her daughter, Sheryl Koch.

Chesnik's scopes tend to be contemporary in style, while

Koch's models veer toward the traditional. One of Sheryl's early designs which still brings a smile is the Bathscope.

Together and apart, this mother-daughter team has grown successful and renowned in the kaleidoscope field. And rightly so — they continually improve their technique, explore new ideas, and add variety to their line of brass and wood kaleidoscopes. They have resisted the urge to "get bigger" and still make each scope in their home-studio and workshop.

They make many adaptations of the basic interchangeable two-wheel scope. Alternate wheels are available with each style. In addition to their traditional German antique, stained glass, Brazilian agate, and textured glass wheels, they also make fused glass wheels and some that embrace a centuries'-old Italian glass-art process — Murrini pattern bar slices wrapped in copper foil.

Janice and Ray are collectors too. Their house is full of works by many of their scope friends. "Looking through them," Janice says, "recalls memories of wonderful times we've shared and the warm associations we've had together, and also reminds us that sometimes our work is play."

Howard Chesshire

Howard Chesshire had an idea for a special kaleidoscope. It was only after experimenting with mirrors and lenses for four years that he learned Sir David Brewster had tested and proved such an instrument more than 150 years earlier. But that didn't bother Howard. He is glad that he didn't realize the telescopic kaleidoscope, as it was originally termed, was already in existence. He had the personal thrill and pleasure of discovering this mandala machine for himself in 1973.

Chesshire strongly believes that the teleidoscope is the purest form of any type of kaleidoscope. "My lens-equipped scope gives the viewer the ability to compose his own image and to change and control it," he says. "I find it particularly gratifying that my artform will continue to create new images and new art even after it leaves my studio."

"The ultimate value of my kaleidoscope is the potential each viewer has to see the artistic value in his own environment," Howard explains. Pointing his scope at a bowl of fresh eggs in his Vermont farm kitchen, Howard told me to look carefully. "Open your other eye," he insisted. "You don't have to close one eye and squint when viewing nature's kaleidoscope."

Chesshire's in good company with his preference for the teleidoscope. He showed me pages 81-85 of the 1858 revised edition of Brewster's Treatise on the Kaleidoscope.

"Without such an extension of power, (referring to the substitution of a lens in place of a cell) the kaleidoscope might only be regarded as an instrument of amusement; but when it is made to embrace objects of all magnitudes, and at all distances, it takes its place as a general philosophical instrument, and becomes of the greatest use in the fine as well as the useful arts...

The patterns which are thus presented to the eye are essentially different from those exhibited by the simple kaleidoscope. Here the objects are independent of the observer, and all their movements are represented with the most singular effect in the symmetrical picture, which is as much superior to what is given by the simple instru-

ment, as the sight of living or moving objects is superior to an imperfect portrait of them."

The "Mandala Kaleidoscope," made in only one model by Chesshire, contains windows, mirrors, lenses, a prism, and a discrete space. The three fine double convex lenses project an image of any object upon the mirrors. Then the image multiplies as it travels through the prism, producing more than 200 reflections of the object in symmetrical patterns. It transforms the objects from your own surroundings into a kinetic montage of vibrant images and inspiring designs. The visual potential is as infinite as the colors and shapes around you.

While "Mandala Kaleidoscopes" are no longer being made by Howard Chesshire, they deserve a place in kaleido-history.

R. Scott Cole

R. Scott Cole has been making kaleidoscopes since 1982. Using the classical Italian process of glassblowing with a torch, Scott is a pioneer in creating scopes entirely of glass. He also uses anodized aluminum encased in blown glass. Flameworked antique glass pieces in the object cells are coordinated with the multicolored round barrels. Due to a special technique, they are lightweight yet durable.

Scott spends as much, or more, of his time teaching others how to make kaleidoscopes. He enjoys sharing what he has learned at workshops and in written projects for books and magazines.

A counselor by profession, Scott Cole continues to explore the connections between personal growth and creativity.

Carmen and Stephen Colley

Carmen and Stephen Colley "reinvented" the wheel when they started designing and making their fabulous two-wheel "found-object" kaleidoscopes. Found objects are personal treasures that have been collected through the years. They are incorporated into wheels that are sensational to look at, but more importantly, the inclusion of items with differing shapes, textures and colors helps create variations of elaborate patterns that do not seem repetitive as in ordinary wheel scopes.

Carmen fell in love with kaleidoscopes at age seven when she traded her favorite yo-yo for a scope. Her fascination has continued, and she becomes so attached to each "new child" that she hates to part with it. When the buyer's enthusiasm matches hers, though (which it usually does), then it's a different story, and she is doubly thrilled.

In their San Antonio garage studio, Carmen and her architect husband, Stephen, make each part of every scope by hand, from the jewelry size scopes to the

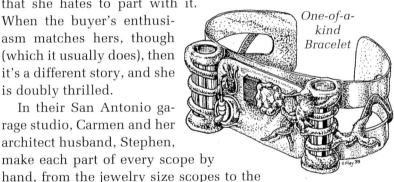

One-of-a-kind Bracelet

pedestal parlor size, and from the beautiful decorative soldering to the hand-painted "Certificate of Content," which details the magic recipe contained in each individually-named scope. To their regular line of kaleidoscope jewelry, Gallocolley Opdesign, their new trade name, is adding a fine silver and gold line of jewelry: "Gold Micron - Beta Series."© They are also in the midst of designing some new models that Carmen says "will not even look like scopes, and some that will not even quite be scopes at all."

David Collier

David Collier says he finally found the right multivalue product to incorporate both his hardwood "feelie" concept and love for kinetic art. As you pick up his eye-catching "Shaker Scope," you will be intrigued by its unique shape and comfortable grip as well as the magical oil-filled interior images. David is especially proud of the smoothness of these precision handcrafted scopes. He uses a large selection of nature's best figured hardwoods.

Peg and Dennis Comeau

Peg and Dennis Comeau of Classical Glass came up with a couple of different twists to the basic wood and glass two-wheel kaleidoscope. Hexagon, cone-shaped viewing tubes made of oak or walnut are lined with six mirrors, and each scope stands on its own built-in foot. Two varying sized color glass wheels spin freely on these hardwood cones. Wheels on other scopes are usually of identical size. This variation, though slight, really gives a different look — quite attractive. Textures and colors are different too.

"Our business is a family one in which friends and relatives help out from time to time. The lifestyle that we are able to lead by living in the country inspires our creativity in bringing visual pleasure to others by way of our scopes. Each time we sell a kaleidoscope to someone, it's like making a new friend — they feel we've put a little joy in their lives, and they take home a part of us in the scope."

Allen and Michele Crandell

Just when I was sure there could be nothing revolutionary about another two-wheel scope, along came Crandell's "Melrose Window." Many scopes resemble rose windows, but this one *is* a rose window. Allen and Michele Crandell are among the most recent additions to the kaleido-family. Like many other scope designers, the Crandells arrived at kaleidoscopes through a series of unexpected circumstances. Health problems dictated a change from the mechanical work for which Allen had been trained.

The Crandell's love for unusual glass is apparent in the large wheels of their stained-glass scopes. They are partial to that which is never to be duplicated, end-of-the-day runs, one-of-a-kind, or limited-production pieces, such as Peter Morris glass.

One wheel in their tall pedestal model (page 115) contains forty-eight slices of different glass. Over 160 pieces of different sizes, colors, and shapes comprise the second wheel. They also make a small "Melrose Window" that is chock full of color and variety. (page 66) Near-black solderwork enhances the centuries-old aura of Crandell's "Melrose Window." Place this scope facing the sun (or a halogen light), very slowly turn the wheels — one at a time, breathe a prayer, and you are in your own private cathedral!

Cliff Crooks

Cliff Crooks of Paso Pottery introduced the first stoneware kaleidoscopes. "Fantasy Laser Lens" was one of the first side-lit scopes and was also among the first to contain a hologram in the lens cap.

Cliff welcomes a challenge and enjoys doing things that are difficult—and different. He was told that a polyangular mirror system couldn't work with a rotating ring. That is the reason a rotating ring is being utilized in his new Raku polyangular scope. Most Raku lusters fade and tarnish, so Cliff found a way to remove the tarnish.

"With experience and knowledge of a few closely guarded secrets," Cliff explains "brilliant lusters can be achieved with every firing. These secrets are the basis for my new business. Raku is an artistic expression of the potter and it is many things to many people. To some, including myself, it is a spiritual experience, but whatever, it's always Zen."

John Culver

John Culver delights in the "kaleidocraze," but doesn't want any part of mass production. Happy and willing to make each part by himself, John cleans his mirrors before starting and polishes each completed product. "The mirror is the heart of the scope, and we are the soul," he says, and refers to scopes as "gentle miracles of reflections."

Strongly attracted to marbles and mirrors, John was among the first to use marbles as the scope's object. He uses them to stunning advantage in "The World Is Your Kaleidoscope." Inspired by Frank Lloyd Wright's architecture, Culver constructed his own architectural sculpture with three venetian glass columns and triangular mirrored walls crowned with a spectacular planet marble by Josh Simpson.

In some of his smaller models, he uses antique sandwich-glass marbles which are indigenous to his part of New England. "The marble acts as a lens," John explains, "and brings in the fisheye image of more than 180 degrees. Why, you can even see behind you."

While John is absorbed with light and vision, he is also fascinated by toys, mystical instruments, and poetry. He equates the following old parable about mirrors to the kaleidoscope:

"They say if you hold a clear glass in front of yourself, you see the world through it, but if you take that piece of glass and put a thin veneer of silver (money) on it, then all you see is yourself.

"I especially like the way this parable relates to kaleidoscopes. Their magic transcends mirrors that reflect your image to mirrors that see inside yourself. This beautiful glimpse, both inward and outward, calms and quiets, relaxes and heals! — it awakens the sleeping dreams and calls them forth!"

As John Culver has watched many kaleidoscopists design

bigger and more elaborate and very expensive scopes, he has decided to go in an opposite direction, switching his talents and attention from leaded glass to papier mâché. What he particularly likes about this medium is its simplicity. John begins by sculpting realistic rocks, stones, and bricks and then inserts a kaleidoscope. A few themes to be developed include Rock of Ages, rock gardens, rock stars, rock & roll, on-the-rocks, stepping stones, birth stones, grave stones, and John's personal favorite, between a rock and a hard place! He also utilizes some of the natural sea shells found along Cape Cod's sandy coast for the body of a few of his special scopes. (see page 67)

A man of strong faith, John confides, "My creativity doesn't come from me, but through me. I see myself as more of an instrument in the creative process. As it passes through me, I affect it as only I can."

Peter and Skeeter DeMattia

Peter and Skeeter DeMattia didn't enter the kaleido-rena until early in 1991, but they are surely making up for lost time. They have already introduced several series of not so ordinary kaleidoscopes. The Warp Factor line includes truncated bodies, containing from one to seven mirrors each.

But it is their Oasis and Bound Images along with the Petite and Grand Illusions that are receiving high plaudits. Uncustomary exteriors and unfamiliar mirror arrangements produce undreamt-of images in these square and rectangular stained glass scopes.

The Oasis is made entirely of dichroic glass and uses a hologram for the third mirror. The glass oil-filled object tube contains tiny multicolored flame-worked twists and pieces. The

"Found Art" Kaleidoscope

pleasing images spiral, pulsate, and well, words don't do it justice — seeing is believing!

The Grand Illusion is an eight by eight inch square of a new thin-rolled art glass resembling slate. The Petite Illusion is a much smaller version, and Bound Images resembles a book with deckled edges. Natural-crystal handles turn the glass object tubes filled with tumbling glass items. A unique mirror arrangement produces a different image. (see page 66)

The DeMattias are experimenting with a "found art" line of scopes. These large one-of-a-kind creations incorporate such unlikely items as an adjustable microphone stand, a brake drum, a five pound weight or a flag pole and use a bicycle gear to turn the object chamber.

Skeeter also designs jewelry items. A necklace with a rectangular body produces a cone-shaped image! Yes, you can count on the DeMattias for the new, the bold, and the beautiful.

Don Doak

Don Doak made his first kaleidoscope as a gift for his son, after picking up Baker's "Through the Kaleidoscope" at a gallery where he delivered the musical jewelry boxes he was making. That was in 1986, and he has been busy making them ever since.

Don's objective is to create a quality kaleidoscope that will be recognizable 100 years from now. Applying all the skills, crafts, and trades he has worked at all his life, Don feels he is achieving this goal. Domed, iridized, stained black glass is Don's trademark style, along with his use of heavily sculptured lead-tin-silver soldering. The "Musical Geodyssey" (page 114) which can be viewed with both eyes, gives the viewer a spectacular image of a slowly moving, bright multifaceted globe or planet suspended in a black void.

Working alone, Don makes every single part of his scopes by hand. He even designs and builds many of his own tools, including a glass cutter capable of cutting a piece of front-surface mirror within 1/1000 of an inch, and a large kiln (including its heating elements).

In 1992, Don's Kaleido-Sphere won the Fifth Brewster Society Award for Creative Ingenuity. (In February 1993, a patent was granted, allowing all 14 claims.) Basically, it involves placing sets of mirrors side by side, mathematically cut so that images converge. In other scopes this produces two different images. In the KaleidoSphere, the more sets of mirrors that are added, the larger the spherical image appears, and the farther away it is viewed, the larger the illusion looms within the sphere (up to a point). So this becomes a scope you look at, rather than into. No matter where you stand, or even if you are walking, the illusion remains constant.

Don's training and heart are in sculpture. He hopes one day to build a really huge KaleidoSphere in a park — a geodesic dome structured of mirrors containing a second inner sculpture of moving light and color.

Notwithstanding the mirror magic and other elements of the kaleidoscope, it is the people he meets that intrigues Don most. He likens the vast spectrum of people to the scope itself. "Perhaps one universal appeal of the kaleidoscope is each individual's innate understanding that we, like the seemingly meaningless pieces of shattered, splintered, imperfect glass in the object box, fit together perfectly to form a more beautiful picture than any one piece ever could by itself; that each of us, flawed as we may be, is essential to the overall mosaic image called humanity."

Sam Douglas

Sam Douglas pays homage to the eternal child in us all with his unique hand-fabricated acrylic scopes.

His mini skyscrapers include the Empire State, Chrysler and Citicorp Buildings. (page 155) Biplanes, rocket ships, and ray guns are among his other-world creations. His newer scope designs have straight, simple lines. "Crystal Phoenix," "Magna Sphere," and "Galaxy Class" are each decorated with swirling hand-painted designs on the rectangular acrylic bodies and front-turning hollow disks. But it is the untypical mirror arrangement (page 66) which creates images that transport you to a magical realm beyond our galaxy!

Sam's experience as a museum director of exhibitions and theatrical set designer stands him in good stead with his "KaleidEscapes." "It still amazes me," he admits, "that such a compact blend of instrument, toy, and artwork offers so much opportunity for individualism and innovation."

Luc and Sallie Durette

Working together in the magical world of kaleidoscopes is a dream realized for Luc and Sallie Durette. The love of art and nature's creations drew them together. In the wilderness of the Pacific Northwest they have found the beauty and serenity that inspire Spectrum Art's creations.

Luc's education in the sciences together with his woodworking and glass skills lends precision and innovation to their limited-edition and one-of-a-kind kaleidoscopes. Sallie contributes her painting, calligraphy and graphic arts skills to their work, along with her lifelong fascination with fantasy and magic.

The Durettes grow and dry the flowers for Pami's Potpourri Kaleidoscopes, dedicated to the memory of Sallie's beloved sister. The aroma of the potpourri along with the floral visuals is an invitation to enter an enchanted secret garden. A Victorian Christmas version with tiny pine cones, wee candy canes and shimmering ornaments amidst the fragrance of bayberry, is reminiscent of an old-fashioned Christmas.

Aurora (the Roman goddess of dawn) is an apt name for both the design and concept of Spectrum Art's top-of-the-line kaleidoscope. The exterior is composed of maple and a special handblown Fremont glass in delicate hues complements the wood perfectly. Two interchangeable barrels can slide into the base, affording a choice of three different mirror systems. Two trays, one lined with black velvet, can hold fresh flowers for summer viewing, autumn leaves for fall, holly and berries for winter or ferns for spring — making this a scope for all seasons. (see photo on page 157) The second tray with a white background accommodates flame-worked glass pieces, shells, and your choice of objects. A third option includes two large wheels which contain, along with stained glass, lace and handpainted silks. More than a year went into the development of this model. Beautifully executed and stunning to behold — the Aurora is a real collection piece for the connoisseur.

Luc and Sallie agree that, "Through our work we hope to provide others with a tool that may be used in the external world to reach that vast and glorious garden within."

Irene and Bill Ecuyer

One of the trimmest and lightest scopes to be found originates in the Vermont home of Irene and Bill Ecuyer. Its calming effect has proven practical application. The Ecuyer's dentist keeps one in his office for patients to enjoy before undergoing treatment.

Before his retirement, Bill was making stained glass lamps and boxes as a hobby. Kaleidoscopes had always interested him, and with more time to experiment, he turned his attention to creating a scope that was in his own words, "different."

Irene and Bill, whose business name is "Bits of the Past," produce two models. One has a wheel with 12 colors and the other contains 24. Making them entirely by hand, they cut the mirrors, cast the old linotype metal wheels and even use their own lathe. After shaping and sealing the 1 x 9 1/2 inch vinyl pieces with heat, they sand and paint them with three coats of flat black paint. Deep intense colors are then imbedded in resin.

Spinning smoothly and swiftly, the small wheels produce images reminiscent of the richly stained glass windows found in European cathedrals.

Mark Eilrich

The "Illusion," by WildeWood Creative Products, provides what many people think is the best image for the least money of any scope available. It is certainly being copied in more various forms than any other scope on the market.

Mark Eilrich is president of WildeWood. It was his wife, Caren, who originated the Space Tubes which are used as the objects to be viewed in the "Illusion." Caren had filled a little tube with beads and water for their daughter to play with. It caught on! In 1983 Mark and Caren started making Space Tubes in their home and, surprisingly, did a landslide business in the first year. Shortly thereafter, Caren was killed in an auto accident. Mark quit his job as a police officer and started his all-American company.

In November 1986, Cozy Baker showed Mark what happened when you put an 18-degree teleidoscope in front of one of his Galaxy Tubes. He immediately agreed that it would make a sensational kaleidoscope. The "Illusion" is but one of many being designed by WildeWood Creative Products.

Marilyn Endress

Marilyn Endress recalls the frustration of loving her childhood kaleidoscope but not knowing the secret of its magic, then her despair when she broke open the casing and was left with only the debris of bits of colored glass and plastic beads.

Whether it was this early experience or the innate creative talents which developed as she matured, Marilyn produces Gemscopes that are beautiful and well made. Her business is aptly named because she uses gems like amethyst crystals, Brazilian and moss agates, carnelian garnets, rose quartz, peridot and faceted Austrian crystals. Optical quality mirrors capture crisp, distortion-free images, and a thin oil in the chamber allows the colors to dance with more alacrity than is usual in many oil-suspension scopes.

Sea shells and swirly glass marbles enhance the finely detailed designs, and butterfly wings and peacock feathers embedded in her two-wheel kaleidoscopes seem to be blown about by colored winds. The brass tube is just different enough in size to be really comfortable to hold, and fits into a neat felt-lined stand. This and the recessed eyepiece are made of Honduran mahogany. The lacquered scope is capped with a leaded crystal to add even more dazzle.

"Creativity, Marilyn says, "has to come from within, you know, before it can be manifested in the outer realm."

Tim and Thea Enos

Tim and Thea Enos (Diversity Glass) designed one variation of the tapered mirror scope that merits mention — a marble scope with a marble at both ends. The wire holding each marble (one large and one small) slides out so that it is viewable from either end. Of course, each view is entirely different so that it is like having two systems in one scope. Diversity Glass was also the first to use Robert Lichtman's spectacular marbles in kaleidoscopes. This started a trend for handblown marbles made especially for scopes.

Dennis and Diane Falconer

Dennis and Diane Falconer had been collecting scopes for several years before Dennis tried his hand at making one as a surprise gift for Diane. The surprise turned out to be for Dennis, though, when he discovered that the real thrill of the scope for him was in making them.

Utilizing both the equipment and skills he used for other hand-blown scientific apparatus, Dennis developed the Ice Cave. (page 70) The entire scope is made of blown glass, both the barrel and objects for the cell, including liquid-filled ampules that Dennis taught himself to make.

Diane's fascination with the Karelitz kaleidoscopes prompted Dennis to turn his attention and talents to polarized-light images. "This image, created by the decomposition of white light into its spectral components, seems to us to be nature's truest form of color," Dennis says. Using a new resin-treated wood for the body, birefringent material in the object cells, and an anodized rotating chamber, Dennis designed two small hand-held scopes: EbonyFire and SappFire.

Newest in the Fire Series is GoldFire, an anodized gold inlaid walnut-bodied scope on a solid walnut pedestal. The pedestal has been formed so that it can also be held by hand. It is accompanied by a matching light box. (page 120)

For Dennis and Diane the most exciting facet of the scope is neither therapy, nor metaphor nor anything else except its just being what it is – a kaleidoscope. To be involved together with an art form that brings them closer to nature's beauty is the true inspiration for the Falconers.

Marti Freund

The first 18-degree two-mirror teleidoscope that ever came to my attention was one made by Marti Freund. That was in 1986, and Marti continues to work with that particular angle in both her teleidoscopes and two-wheel kaleidoscopes.

Every single piece used in Marti's scopes is handcrafted. Even the brass washers used between the wheels, and a tension washer designed to keep tension on the wheels (so that they will not freewheel) are handtooled by Marti's father, Edmond Freund. He also makes the metal jigs to aid in soldering the wheels.

The sleek bodies of these scopes are made of antique mirror or iridescent stained glass. To many, Marti adds decorative filigree and scratchings. The latter technique is one Marti developed. "Scratching is just like it sounds," Marti explains. "I scratch a design out of the back side of the glass and then I add color to it."

Filigrees of animals and birds convey Marti's interest in the world. "If by looking at my elephant or hummingbird or other animal filigree, someone might be influenced to enjoy and respect our wildlife more, that would be the greatest accomplishment I could ever want."

Mike Gallick

Mike Gallick designed the original glass-rod kaleidoscopes (not to be confused with other peoples' prepackaged kits). He makes both a marble scope with interchangeable handblown marbles and a wheelscope with fused and painted glass wheels. The sleek, transparent barrel is made of clear glass rods with a colorful painting visible beneath the glass.

Steven Gray

Steven Gray was the recipient of the Sixth Brewster Society Award for Creative Ingenuity. Each of the first five awards was given for a particular scope by an individual artist. In the case of Gray & Gray Woodwrights, the award was presented to Steven for his cumulative conceptual contribution to the kaleidoscene. Close to a dozen major works combine Steven's matchless woodworking skill with his unparalleled mirror configurations.

Steven enjoys the function and feel that old instruments and tools possess and strives to improve on their design. As a child, he spent time in his grandfather's workshop. He has also always had an interest in optics and light. Kaleidoscopes offered a perfect solution for combining these two interests. His designs are an up-to-the-minute interpretation of instruments designed in the past.

The pieces that Steven turns take their form from the piece of wood at hand. The shape of the burl and its natural contours determine the shape and edge. The wood that he uses tends to be from the root area, a burl, a crotch of a limb or an area of the tree where a fungus has discolored the wood or caused a thin black line (spalting). In short, the wood Steven uses would not be considered good quality for lumber. Yet it will yield some of the most fascinating pieces of art. The comment is often made that his kaleidoscopes have a Jules Verne look and, indeed, certain styles do imply that an adventure is about to begin.

Different in concept from other scopes, "The Carousel" features a revolving turntable, suspended from a frame with three brass cables. The array of items that can be displayed is limitless. (Be sure to try adding a holographic disk and fresh flowers.) Interchangeable and reversible fabric pads add background color and design. The barrel is removable and can be used as a teleidoscope. There are two different signed limited editions of 30 each.

"Chamber Extenuation" is one of his most artistically imaginative pieces. In this walnut and ebony scope, the background color as well as the 17-point star images can be changed. Twelve interchangeable glass slides, each of different colored and patterned glass, fit neatly into the base of the scope. A separate mirror acts as a light source for "Chamber Extenuation".

Two of Steven's newest and most optically inspired scopes afford a view as though you were inside the mirror system, or viewing from the side of the scope. In "Geocentrical Dream" the image appears to be a sphere within a sphere. Two cells control the patterns, one for each sphere. Made of black walnut, it is a limited edition of 25.

"Espy from Within" is viewed from the side rather than from the end of the scope and contains two cells creating an image which appears to be two cylinders. The view is strong, close to the eye, and appears to extend into a dark void. Limited edition of 25.

Steven says, "Kaleidoscopes do not seem to attract a singular group or personality type, but rather are enjoyed by young and old, the quiet and the boisterous, the non-affluent and the well-to-do. Nearly every person is excited by a scope's captivating powers."

Stan Griffith

"...And on the Eighth day. Kaleidoscopes." That is the name of Stan Griffith's kaleidoscope company. Being a pipe fitter and heli-arc welder, not an artist, Stan hadn't thought about kaleidoscopes at all, much less as a career, until the summer of 1988.

His ornate stained-glass kaleidoscopes

with decorative soldering attest to the fact that he learns fast and has latent artistic talents.

Stan uses handblown marbles as the viewing objects for his handsome scopes. He was the first to use an egg-shaped marble and to put two marbles in the same scope. Stan has recently introduced an elaborate parlor scope that contains three marbles in the objective end. (page 66)

"I think when Sir David Brewster completed the first kaleidoscope," Stan chuckles, "God must have been looking over his shoulder and said, 'Yes!!'"

Gregory Hanks

When Gregory Hanks was a boy, his favorite toy was an airplane. He had airplanes everywhere, even hanging from the ceiling. Much of his childhood was spent creating new and challenging models.

The turning point toward kaleidoscopes started in 1987, when he read "Through the Kaleidoscope," by Cozy Baker. "Kaleidoplanes" put dreams and fantasy into flight. They are mythical planes designed to fly in the midst of jeweled rainbows. Made of stained glass and brass, "Jewels in the Air Collection" enclose the highest quality optics. Viewing cells and propellers are designed to fit the theme, optics, and overall enhancement of the plane. Each piece is individually handcrafted and finely detailed, then plated in silver, brass, or copper and finished to a high polish. (see page 184)

There are currently nine models in the line, including a hot-air balloon, and Greg is currently building a helicopter with an all new design in optics. All series in the "Jewels in the Air Collection" are engraved, limited editions.

"Kaleidoscopes are ageless, " Greg says, "because they hold a new world of balanced exploration. They can be appreciated by young and old, rich and poor and have no language, ethnic, nor religious barriers."

James Dana Hill

James Hill's real interest was triggered when he saw a collection of modern kaleidoscopes in an art gallery. What made those scopes so interesting to James was how eye-catching the external designs were. "Even before looking through them," he states, "there was this unique, intriguing mystery about them. Then there was the mystery of the images themselves, because I didn't know then what optical magic was at work."

One of the surprising factors to James is the fact that every single kaleidoscope has its own different personality. He makes a conscious effort to try to improve each scope and to study what makes some better than others. The two styles of kaleidoscope that James Hill makes are uniquely his own. One is fitted into a cane (KaleidoCane) and the keyed kaleidoscopes are operated by pressing musical-type brass keys.

For James, as for many of the artists, the kaleidoscope's therapy is in the making of them. "It's a visual rendition of music — some scopes are Johann Strauss; some are John Philip Sousa. The images pass through the eye and straight to the heart." James adds, "I'm working on something that will take you all the way into the image. I think that's the future direction of scopes."

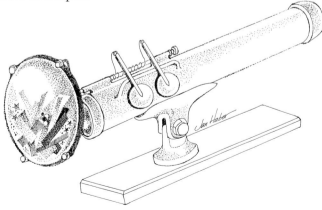

Amy Hnatko

While Amy Hnatko (silent H) received an M.A. from the University of Pittsburgh and has taken postgraduate courses at various other universities, in her field of stained glass she is largely self-taught. This was accomplished by extensive reading and traveling. She scoured Great Britain and Europe studying the great cathedrals and churches.

A deep sense of play is the basis of Amy's urge to create. She loves to experiment with new media such as wood, fiber, and clay, incorporating what she learns into her glass work.

Although Amy doesn't condone kaleidoscopists "borrowing" ideas from her work or that of other artists, neither does she think that one should expend too much energy in anger if this should occur. Rather, she suggests that any "anger should be channeled into energies that are constructively creative." Some of her best new scopes, it seems, have come about after someone had "adopted" one of her earlier creations.

"Imagine combining the joy of a child at play with the challenge of physics," Amy muses, "and you'll get an idea of what I experience when designing a new kaleidoscope. The principles of physics underlie my decisions on how to build sculptures that are sturdy while appearing to be delicate."

Amy has always had a passion for fountains and has struggled to combine stained glass and flowing water, first in windows and wall hangings and more recently in a kaleidoscope. The whole idea for the "Fountain Scope" (see Page 117) unfolded to Amy in such detail that she cut and built most of it without any plans.

Northern Lights have been described as a veil or scarf of shimmering color streaking across the sky. This effect is achieved in Amy's kaleidoscope, "Northern Lights," with clear, ripple glass. (Page 180) The objects are special glass globes into which ephemeral colors are blown and then filled with liquid. The floating objects might be as unusual as hand-dyed, unspun wool fibers, as fragile as cicada wings, and as sturdy as sterling silver stars. This piece is a limited edition of 10.

"The urge to create is a mysterious companion, sometimes so intrusive as to be an exhausting taskmaster, at other times disappearing altogether for unpredictable periods."

Craig Hopkins

In creating "Nature's Image" kaleidoscopes, Craig Hopkins says, "To capture nature's image on a camera, it's a snap of the shutter. With my scopes, it's a turn of the wrist." In his Looking Glass Series, Craig fills the Pyrex glass bodies, as well as the hemispherical turning lens, with assorted crystals, semiprecious stones, feathers, autumn leaves, sea shells, and many more of Earth's treasures. He hand turns exotic wooden stands to hold each scope.

"Night Vision Wandscope" is one of the most interesting of the numerous variations on the "Illusion" concept. The back mirror is a holographic mylar that divides the light spectrum into rainbows of color creating a perpetual fireworks display. The handblown Pyrex glass body is hand painted and a small flashlight serves as a handle as well as for inner light.

Annie & Craig Huber

There wasn't any formal period of research and design for Annie and Craig Huber. In school, Craig was one of those kids who were constantly doodling geometric shapes on their class papers. Clearly, those patterns and ten years of experimenting with stained glass and mirrors provided him with an important base of information.

Dividing the tasks of designing, manufacturing, assembling and shipping, the Hubers have transformed their fascination with glass and geometry into a flourishing cottage industry. Annie and Craig feel strongly about the benefits of forming and operating an enterprise where the lines between work and home, business and pleasure have been mostly erased. So their lifestyle is wrapped up in kaleidoscopes — even their neighbors are involved and everyone's happy. "It's a natural blend of our individual passion for geometric symmetry and creative self-expression. We view the kaleidoscope as 'meditation for the eye'," Craig says.

Galaxy Glass works offers a wide variety of scopes in a choice of leather or decorator fabrics. The Galactiscope is a real eye-teaser with a cascade of dazzling tubular reflections that swirl right up to the eye. One of their most popular models is the "Create-a-Scope," in which a removable plastic end cap allows a refill of any objects at all. Left unfilled, it becomes a see-through scope. Then there is a nature scope that contains tiny treasures like bits of agate and lacy mosses from their homeland, the Oregon wilderness.

Deb Jerison

Deb Jerison has found kaleidoscopes to be fun ever since she received both a scope and a large prism in her Christmas stocking at the age of eight. She took the scope apart immediately and carried the prism with her every place, holding it to her eye and enjoying all the contorted views of the world around her.

Deb still feels the kaleidoscope's main function is fun. To prove it, she has come up with a couple of novel stained glass versions: one with a decorative paddle wheel as the viewing object, and another that uses an air-filled bellows to blow the bits and pieces about.

Doug Johnson

Creating from images that well up from his inner experiences, Doug Johnson was not only a precursor in the kaleidoscope explosion, but is an innovative designer who first introduced many of the styles and concepts being embellished today.

He remembers that as a child, he fell in love with the remnants of a local industry — costume jewelry. The brightly colored glass and plastic that frequently dusted the sidewalks captured his attention. So did the stained glass windows in

church, "where my mind wandered...enjoying the music and admiring the colors...," he reminisces.

These were just the beginnings of an aesthetic awareness for Doug, whose formal background of math, psychology, and computer science has come back full circle to that of color and image.

It was only a matter of time until Doug merged his scientific world into his colorful dream world. More than ten years ago while working with computers, he visited a local arts and crafts show. An exhibit of stained glass recaptured his early fascination. He saw a way of living the dreams he loved while at the same time creating something tangible. By 1977, Doug abandoned computers and worked full-time with stained glass. In 1978, he came out with his first kaleidoscope.

Doug takes great pride in his special contributions to the growing art of kaleidoscopy, and rightly so. His influence and list of "firsts" is impressive. As Doug points out, his early method of combining kevels (his own term for his copyrighted glass object cases) with elongated triangular mirrored bodies soldered with copper may not seem so distinctive now that many others are employing the same technique. Realizing that the inner image is the most crucial part of a scope, Doug was among the first to use front-surface mirrors in all his designs.

First to use clear and beveled glass for the body of the scope, he then designed and developed the kevel, using stained glass materials and techniques. One of his innovations was a kevel that could be opened, thus enabling "each person to control his own kaleidoscope experience," by putting in special objects and favorite colors. For even more variety, Doug introduced interchangeable kevels and wheels, and double combinations thereof.

The ability to "personalize" the kaleidoscope to the viewer's liking is important to Doug, since he wants people to be able to sample and enjoy as much of the infinite variety of styles, textures, and colors as possible.

To his credit also goes the first marble scope. When high quality latticinio marbles are rotated at the end of the tube, streams of color bounce off the inner mirrors to create myriad patterns. New on the market is his adapter, which accommodates a range of various sized marbles in the same scope.

Highly original and singularly his own, the binocular kaleidoscope joins two viewers which focus on one set of wheels. Doug has several versions of this bi-scope, one of which includes a special mirror that allows pastel tinted images to enter the visual field through the body of the scope. The blending of these images with those entering through the end piece creates highly sophisticated and multidimensional images of extraordinary colors — it's like a technicolor map of fairyland. This he calls his "Super Binoc."

Maximizing the kaleidoscope's playfulness, Doug offers more than 30 different sizes, shapes, and styles. Satellite and roller scopes are two of his newer styles. The "Carousel" is a combination of the two. The "Scopeitall" is a table model with a rotating tray on which you can view any of your favorite jewelry or other goodies.

Referring again to the images, Doug says, "Images in kaleidoscopes are nonverbal, not linked to words, or to anything at all. Things may come and go, but kaleidoscope images once viewed are with us forever."

Denise Jones

Denise Jones has been making and selling kaleidoscopes since 1983. Her styles are many and varied, but in most she combines stained glass with oak. A tall tripod floor model with a six mirror system is one of her most distinctive items. Other popular models include a music box, the Art Deco Lady collection (see page 155), and a new line of multicolored alabaster-stone scopes.

David Kalish

David Kalish is a gentleman of many talents. Fascination with illusion led him to the theatre, but an incessant inner tugging drew him back to the visual arts, which he has enjoyed from the earliest time he can remember. David finds the kaleidoscope an exciting new canvas upon which to paint.

Many Chromoscopes are made of acrylic and are truly modern in design. One model, Chromoscope II, combines elements of both the kaleidoscope and teleidoscope. It displays the foreground and background simultaneously, providing a three-dimensional effect. The hemispheric lens turns objects of the immediate outside environment into oblong images.

The triangular reflecting prism refracts this captured light into a continuously changing pattern of symmetrical forms. Simultaneously, bits and pieces tumble before the prism at random in a constantly changing metamorphosis of brilliant kaleidoscopic visions. The cap at the end is removable so that you can add your own bits of whimsy. Try a few kernels of popped corn — it's wild.

One of the most popular of all the Chromoscopes is the "Wedding Kaleidoscope" — a marriage of two scopes blended into one. Looking through opposite ends, two people can view together, yet each will witness a uniquely different vision as each side contains a different mirror system (one prismatic, the other square).

David Kalish believes that the most intriguing aspect of the kaleidoscope is its ability to produce, in infinite variation, designs of perfect symmetry. He feels that there is something deep within our nature that universally responds to this impeccable order of symmetry. "In symmetry there is balance; in balance there is harmony; in harmony, equilibrium. As long as we are perfectly balanced, we cannot fall. As long as we do not fall, we continue to survive. Survival is the ultimate and perpetual striving of all living things — from the most primitive to the most sophisticated being. Somewhere therein lies the relationship between the universal appeal of kaleidoscope mandalas, the inspiration of beauty, the wonder of nature, and the awesome magnificence of Creation itself."

Chromoscopes say it all again and again.

Charles Karadimos

Charles Karadimos began working with glass in 1975 and has focused his work on kaleidoscopes exclusively since 1979. Even in those early days Charles was concerned with exploring and developing mirror systems with different angles and perfect optics that would produce unusual and intricate images.

Over the years, Charles' work has evolved through a natural progression of refinements and improvements — pioneering some of the most significant developments in kaleidoscope art. Each new style that he designs contains a different mirror configuration, which means the points in the starlike images range from four to fourteen.

Using a balance of colors, shapes and textures, Charles personally selects and handworks each piece for the object chamber. The glass bits are cut, melted and flame-worked to yield an interior image that perfectly complements the exterior. He also continues to develop his fusing and slumping techniques, creating scopes that are pleasing to the touch as well as to the eye. They vary in length from three to twenty-four inches.

Charles has always worked alone. He makes each part and component by hand and there are no machined or mass-produced parts. Each scope is an original, signed and numbered piece of art built to last a lifetime. According to the artist, "The exterior draws you in and the interior holds you there."

Judith Karelitz

Judith Karelitz was a vanguard of the kaleidoscope renaissance, with a patent granted in 1974. Inspired by antique kaleidoscopes as a child, Judy determined that someday she was going to make the most beautiful kaleidoscope in the world. And she was convinced that she did just that when she designed the very first modern plexiglass kaleidoscope utilizing polarized light.

Studying the very theories of light polarization advanced by Brewster, Judy probed and experimented until she realized her vision. "I was totally obsessed and possessed when I evolved the "Karelitz Kaleidoscope," the New York artist admitted. "I have never been so completely involved and dedicated in my life, and when in September of '71 the Karelitz Kaleidoscope appeared at The New York Museum of Modern Art, it was like a dream come true."

Totally today in structure, yesterday in appeal, and tomorrow in concept, the exterior of this limited signed edition of 100, is as unique as the interior. Tall and sleek, the clear column of plexiglass contains a hollow red transparent prism in place of mirrors. Colorless pieces of doubly refracting material ebb and flow in fluid, creating imagery that is distinctly different from any other scopes anywhere. Since no colored glass is used, only polarized light, the colors are different too. Purples and magentas float in and out of soft pastels.

Here is the way Judy described it: "Ordinary white light which vibrates in all directions is polarized along one plane when it passes through the base of the tube. The light then enters clear, colorless pieces of birefringent material and is reorganized by the eyepiece to produce the startling colors that you see. These color combinations are completely unique, except, perhaps, sometimes one might see such colors in a garden — but with more opacity."

At the request of the Museum of Modern Art, Judy developed the "Karascope", a patented, inexpensive variation of her limited edition. "Karascope I" proved such a success that the Smithsonian Institute in Washington, D.C. commissioned a Karascope II. These two designs, produced in large numbers, remain two of her most popular models.

An outstanding feature inherent in Judy's polarized light scopes, and exclusively hers, is the turning mechanism. With a twist of the end piece, the design changes. Turn the eyepiece and only the colors change. Turn them both and voilà! The interior world changes. Asymmetrical images of the spectral colors of light itself drift and float like billowing clouds and undulating rainbows. They are in marked contrast to the more traditional geometric symmetry viewed in the average scope.

Another special characteristic of the Karelitz scopes is their ability to shine on cloudy days. Most kaleidoscopes are activated by the sun or artificial light, but for viewing polarized light scopes, gray skies are even better than blue.

Judy's award-winning sculpture and photographs convey her intimate sense of nature. As she put it, "In my work I have tried to encapsulate my deep connection with nature by translating the natural and physical phenomena found there — water, sky, ocean, earth, rainbows, flowers, pebbles, rocks — into mutable self-contained forms. I like to think of my involvement with nature as a joining — as though I am putting my signature on nature."

When I asked Judy what she had in mind for the future, she

said, "As long as I can remember, I've visualized a tall scope like the Karelitz Kaleidoscope which would project images on the ceiling. I would still love to create such a sculpture."

This dream was not to be, because this talented sculptress, photographer, and artist died of cancer in 1987. She will always be remembered in the kaleidoworld as a true master of light, shape, and color.

Dean Kent

Dean Kent was the partner of Stephen Auger during the mid-80s. Then he and his wife, Mary, started making their own line of scopes under the name Living Design. One of their most popular is "Precious Cygnet" necklace, a classic little scope with a neat design and a great image. It was one of the first jewelry scopes to contain the two-mirror system. Dean's kaleidoscope philosophy is explained on page 47.

Randy and Shelley Knapp

Randy and Shelley Knapp don't just produce kaleidoscopes ... they seem to breathe life into them. Combining Randy's skills as a glass cutter and wood artist with Shelley's glass sculpting ability and eye for color has brought about some remarkable kaleidoscopes.

Randy's favorite aspect of scope-making is designing new models. Attesting to this fact is the large number, to date, of their limited edition scopes, including but not confined to: "Dichro-Vision," "Falling Star," "Star Jumper," "Talon," "Reflections of Friendship," (in collaboration with Sherry Moser), "Dream Quest," "Fly By," and "Kalos."

Shelley says her favorite aspect of kaleidoscopery is meeting all the wonderful people at the Brewster Society conventions, exhibitions, and regional meetings. "The groups of artists, collectors and shop owners are as varied and beautiful as the kaleidoscopes themselves," she states.

Eminently successful in blending optical engineering and sculpted art into functional beauty, Randy and Shelley are ever looking toward new horizons, new experiences and new designs. They were among the first to use a black-backdrop, side-lit object cell. In fact, "Twilight," the name of their first scope using that type of cell, has become almost a generic term for the black background image.

Novel or classic, important or small, the Knapps put their heart and soul into each piece, so that their work will endure through generations of appreciative collectors.

Ken and Cheryl Kosage

Love of their Colorado outdoors and a fascination with the effects of light prisms moved Ken and Cheryl Kosage into the scope field and has kept them there. Although the Kosages are now represented in galleries throughout the country, it is still the one-to-one association with the customers that they enjoy.

Doing what came naturally to them, Ken and Cheryl first developed a scope using dried wild flowers. This brings to mind a reference made in a French magazine shortly after Brewster invented the Scope. It said, in part, that the Chinese, who were familiar with this wonderful instrument, called it a wan-boa-tang, which means "tube of a thousand flowers."

The Kosages design and make their own ceramic tubes. This is one of the few ceramic scopes, and they use it for their dried-flower and stained-glass wheels as well as Austrian crystal gazing balls and nuggets. A hand-oiled select-wood stand cradles each handheld scope, even the tiny model. They also make a large parlor scope, the "Galileo."

The Kosages have a deep respect for tradition, and they are hoping customers will come to think of their scope as an heirloom to be passed down. "We live in a world that is so 'on the go' that if we can play a small part in exposing people to a time gone by when people were more content with simple beauties, then we will feel a continued growth from our art."

Dean Krause

Dean Krause experiments with many different types of kaleidoscopes. He doesn't like to keep making one style very long. But one line of scopes that his customers won't let him stop making is the wearable art jewelry. In many of these scopes the eyepiece is heart-shaped.

One piece (1/4" in diameter and 1" long) can be worn either as a ring or a pendant. Complete with a turning end, it gives a very good image. But, without a doubt, the best image seen in a miniature scope appears in Dean's earrings — or more accurately, earring, since the set includes a scope for one ear and a dangling abstract chunk of mirror for the other. The triangular mirrored and copper-soldered body is one and three-quarter inches long. At the end of each is a tiny brass wheel embedded with bits of colored glass. Tapered mirrors produce a sphere image which is made surprisingly clear by the addition of a magnifying lens. These can also be made into pins and tie tacks.

In sharp contrast, Dean makes a large floor model scope. Recently he has started working with acrylic and to many of his newer pieces he adds silver animal figures and other of nature's creatures.

Dean often takes time away from scope-making to travel in Central America, where he finds inspiration in the rain forests and the ancient cultures of the Mayan and Olmec people.

Ron Kuhns

A unique feature of Ron Kuhns' scopes is the fact that the object cells contain three-dimensional opaque objects rather than translucent ones. These are enhanced by the reflective colors of dichroic glass. A few include a self-contained light source. In addition to over thirty types of exotic and domestic woods, Ron makes one limited-edition model of elk's horn. (see page 64)

With more and more artists making larger and more expensive scopes, it is refreshing to see Ron making a smaller scope with a budget price-tag. Crafted from solid maple and painted with graphite, the "Meteor" has a titanium eyepiece and stands on rose quartz or hematite feet.

Kathy Lawson and Landon Seelig

In one of the most unique models originated at Dream Factory, Kathy Lawson and Landon Seelig converted a triangular leaded-glass kaleidoscope into the shape of an old biplane with the interchangeable hand-painted wheels forming a double propeller. Not only is the Skyscope an amusing conversation piece, but the optics are good, and both their geometric cut glass and abstract painted wheels provide vivid and varying images.

The Dream Factory is a concept that Kathy has had for a long time. "I want to have the capability to create anything that can be dreamed of," she explains.

This handful of sparkling colors are certain to catch the eye and dull the appetite. Available in five flavors: cinnamon, lemon-lime, plum, blueberry, and rainbow sherbet, Hard Candy comes with a Kaleidoscope Diet:

1. Eat three balanced meals a day.
2. Exercise wisely.
3. When you feel the urge to snack, pick up sugar-free, non caloric "Hard Candy" and spin the wheels till hunger subsides.

Jack Lazarowski
Tim Grannis

Jack Lazarowski and Tim Grannis (Prism Designs) are probably best known for the Geoscope. If not the first, they were certainly among the very first to use tapered mirrors to create the image of a perfect sphere. Their large floor model has been used by many to photograph the world in kaleidoscopic perspectives.

Tim is first of all a sculptor, then a jeweler. Jack worked as an industrial and graphic designer before he started building gold and silver flutes and piccolos. From there he moved into jewelry. Together they make jewel-like music in the form of participatory sculptural teleidoscopes.

The "Gallery" is a sculptural assemblage of five teleidoscopes, each with a different optical image and removable from a lighted base. In addition to their state-of-the-art teleidoscopes, Prism Designs made one kaleidoscope, "Metaphor." Sleekly modern, yet graceful in design, the glass sparkles and the gold and chrome plated brass shines. (page 154)

Being of the opinion that the scope should be handsome, not merely a cylinder that comes alive only when looked through, Jack and Tim put it this way: "We like seeing the kaleidoscope as a way of encouraging people to look at their environment in a slightly different way."

Ron and Claudia Lee

For many years, Ron and Claudia Lee of the Laughing Coyote had been creating a variety of contemporary wooden items which incorporated flowers and weeds. One day, a customer asked if they could make a kaleidoscope with flowers, and they were immediately embarked on a new venture. They soon discovered that their customers showed greater interest in scopes than in any of their other products.

The Laughing Coyote's representation in the scope field indicates that they have met their objective — beauty and quality at affordable prices. Ron and Claudia continue to experiment, adding new models on a regular basis.

The floral scope continues to be one of the most popular of their line, especially the mini model. Ron executes the hardwood cases, and Claudia takes care of the flowers which are dried and then cast in a resin compound. Some of the wheels contain delicate ferns and Queen Anne's lace. Others are filled with rose petals and pansies or wildflowers along with tiny Victorian faces, fans and other bits of nostalgia. Wheels are interchangeable, so you can plant your own scope garden.

The Lees derive great satisfaction from public reaction to their scopes, especially children's. Two items that remain perennial favorites are geared to children: the Kidoscope, a small wooden scope with a leather carrying strap that looks like a slingshot, and the Treasure Scope, an upright scope which comes with a "viewer dish" and a bag of "tumbles" (dried flowers, stones and assorted colorful trinkets). The fun is being able to substitute your own shells, jewels, and other treasures.

Dorothea (Thea) Marshall

It was while tutoring learning-disabled children in the early 70s that Dorothea Marshall hit upon the idea to recreate one of her favorite childhood toys — a kaleidoscope. She had the kids construct scopes using toilet paper tubes for the casing. Later she made scopes for gifts using better materials; and before she knew it, she was in business.

"Nobody was selling truly handmade scopes when I started," Dorothea explains. "I made each piece myself and then took them to shows and sold them, and they weren't easy to sell either, because people in those days thought of a kaleidoscope as a cheap toy, not an art object."

Having helped pioneer the return of the handcrafted kaleidoscope to the American craft scene, Dorothea pushed the frontiers a little further by spearheading (with her husband, scientist Dr. Ethan Allen) a three-year traveling exhibit, "Kaleidoscopes: Reflections of Science and Art" for the Smithsonian Institution Traveling Exhibition Service.

Dorothea has ceaselessly pressed for high quality in the field. Her chapter in Thom Boswell's *The Kaleidoscope Book* deals with the need for novice and professional artists alike to consider issues ranging from safety to ethics. She has also designed and produced a quality kit to accompany that book.

This energetic lady continues to blaze new trails as she uses kaleidoscope creation to enhance art and self-esteem among "at-risk" school children in Chicago's Urban Gateways program. "Working with this organization is both exhilarating and draining," Dorothea admits, "but I do believe that enriching the lives of inner-city children with the joys and harmonies of kaleidoscopes will surely help make the world a better place."

Leslie Martin
Sabina Diehr

Soul Spectacles came into being as a result of "childhood memories, an old *Scientific American* article, and research ending with a call to a lady named Cozy Baker." Then, one look through that first handcrafted tube and Leslie Martin and Sabina Diehr were "hooked."

The apartments they had while in medical school and during residency were too small for Sabina to continue ceramics or for Leslie to build guitars and harpsichords, but kaleidoscopes on the carpet was just about right (although they eventually worked on the kitchen table and ate on the floor).

Proving that the busiest people find the most time for new tasks and interests, Leslie and Sabina, while both practicing full time as doctors, have managed to make three different series of kaleidoscopes.

"Oracle" and "Meteor" are both stained-glass scopes which can be opened to admit additional objects. One model comes with interchangeable clear and black endpieces. This was the first scope I ever saw with a black backdrop. It was in 1989, and at that time the only scopes with a black background, to my knowledge, were the ones using polarized light. Theirs was also one of the first to use side lighting (this allows the use of nontransparent objects without losing the 3-D effect).

"Meteor" produces the image of a sphere floating in space. Leslie is especially thrilled with the optical illusion of looking down into the icosahedron of the "Meteor," yet seeing the outside of a polyhedron.

Thanks to more space in Wisconsin, Leslie and Sabina have been able to combine an old passion for pottery with their continuing craze for scopes. "Turkish Knightz" is reminiscent of mysterious minarets encountered on their extensive travels. (page 114) "The image is a night sky nova of colors," Sabina explains. "And as far as we know, ours are the first scopes to be thrown on a wheel."

Don McClure

Melding space-age technology (dichroic glass) with turn-of-the-century stained-glass construction technique (Tiffany style), Don McClure creates scopes reminiscent of the art deco era.

Don explored the magic of kaleidoscopes on a part-time basis when he worked full-time as an engineer and a project manager at the Jet Propulsion Laboratory in California. There he was involved in the American space program to explore the mysteries of deep space before retiring in 1989.

Don was the first to write a book on how to make a kaleidoscope. In "Kaleidoscope Magic" (out of print) Don describes how to make his own adaptation of a tapered two-wheel scope.

Earl McNeil

It was after major surgery for a brain tumor that Earl McNeil's interest in the arts and creative crafts was rekindled. He set out to integrate the very best aspects of kaleidoscopes with what he knew of the physics and chemistry of polarized light and the psychology of vision.

Using his woodworking skills, Earl makes the barrels for his Polarascopes. Since it takes very bright light to realize the full potential of polarized light, Earl added a built-in light to his parlor Polarascope.

Teaching is Earl's first priority of business, and he no longer makes very many scopes. His name, however, is one of the first, after the late Judith Karelitz, to be associated with polarized-light kaleidoscopes.

Bob McWilliam

Kaleidoscopes are a retirement profession for Bob McWilliam. The biggest challenge of his new enterprise was to develop an original design. "With so many different styles already out there, what could I come up with that would be distinctive?" Bob asked. Everyone who owns a McWilliam scope will attest to its distinctiveness.

Bob names each of his one-of-a-kind kaleidoscopes individually and provides a personal card of authenticity. Each signed and numbered scope is crafted in stained glass on a matching sculptured hardwood base. He makes both two- and three-mirror scopes. Built into the stand is a hidden compartment to hold a treasure-trove of tidbits to interchange with the viewing pieces inside the object cell. These include liquid-filled ampules that Bob makes himself.

"I find the creative process of designing scopes very fulfilling," Bob says, "and it is pleasing to me to have people enjoy and appreciate what I've created."

Barbara Mitchell

Whatever Barbara Mitchell turns her talents toward can be counted on to win an award. Barbara received her first award at the age of 13, when she was chosen winner of a doll-making contest sponsored by UNICEF and *Seventeen* Magazine. Eleanor Roosevelt and ballerina Margot Fonteyn were among the distinguished judges and while in New York to receive the award, Barbara appeared on the Ed Sullivan Show and the Dave Garroway Today Show.

Winning a scholarship to attend life drawing classes at Chouinard Art Institute in Los Angeles is what really influenced the direction of Barbara's artistic endeavors. A research paper entitled "Psychology of Color" triggered her quest for knowledge on how color, light, sound, and shapes affect our bodies and emotions and health in general. Painting and experimenting with kaleidoscopes have been Barbara's chief interests since she gave up the frantic pace of commercial and residential interior design.

Elevating the kaleidoscope to an instrument for healing and inner peace as well as providing inspirational entertainment has been her goal for several years.

In 1986, Barbara Mitchell won the Second Brewster Society Award for Creative Ingenuity for her SpectraSphere™. This is a projection kaleidoscope which is equipped with a two-mirror lens system that is polyangular, giving the viewer an endless variety of intricate patterns. It can also project images from a wide range of different types of cells, including oil-filled, free-tumbling, and polarized cells, as well as cells containing transparencies.

Imagery can be projected on a traditional flat screen up to 20 feet in diameter. A 24" rear-screen projection dome pro-

(continued on page 121)

Pat Kehs holds cell used to project polyangular images through SpectraSphere
Top three images from Robin Hanson's floral transparency
Large Image from cell by Barbara Mitchell

"Musical Geodyssey" by Don Doak

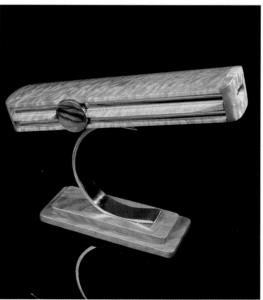

"Turkish Knightz" by Leslie Martin and Sabina Diehr

"Collaboration" by Corki Weeks and Henry Bergeson

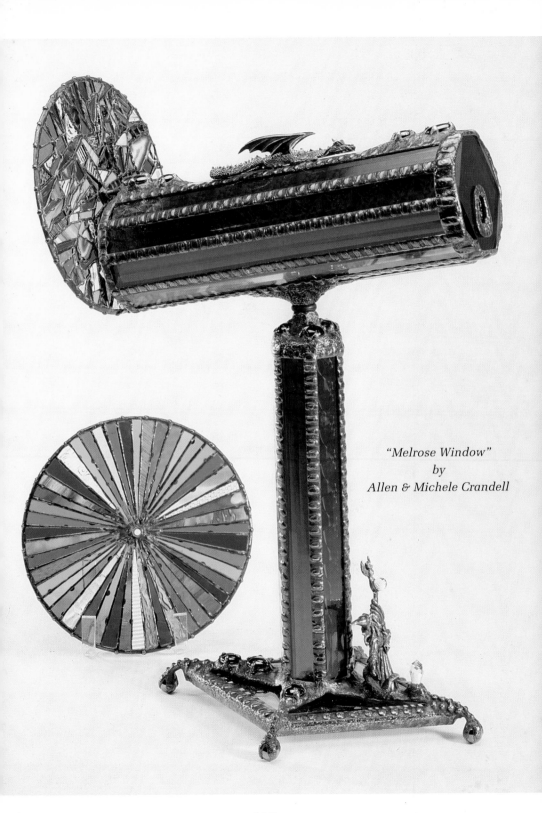

"Melrose Window"
by
Allen & Michele Crandell

*"Home Planet," polyangular scope by
Willie Stevenson. The viewing object is
a 5" handblown marble by Shantidevi.*

Foreword by
Jacques-Yves Cousteau

The Home Planet

Kelley/ASE

The Home Planet

Conceived and edited by
Kevin W. Kelley
For the Association
of Space Explorers

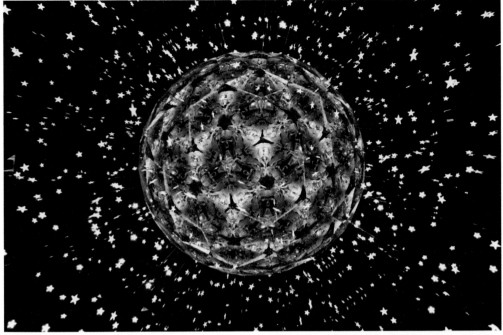

"Journey" image by Sherry Moser   *The "Fountain of Light" by Amy Hnatko*

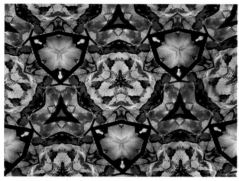

Nelson Poe

Parman Brothers

Gemini Kaleidoscopes

Don Doak

Scopes and image by
Randy and Shelley Knapp

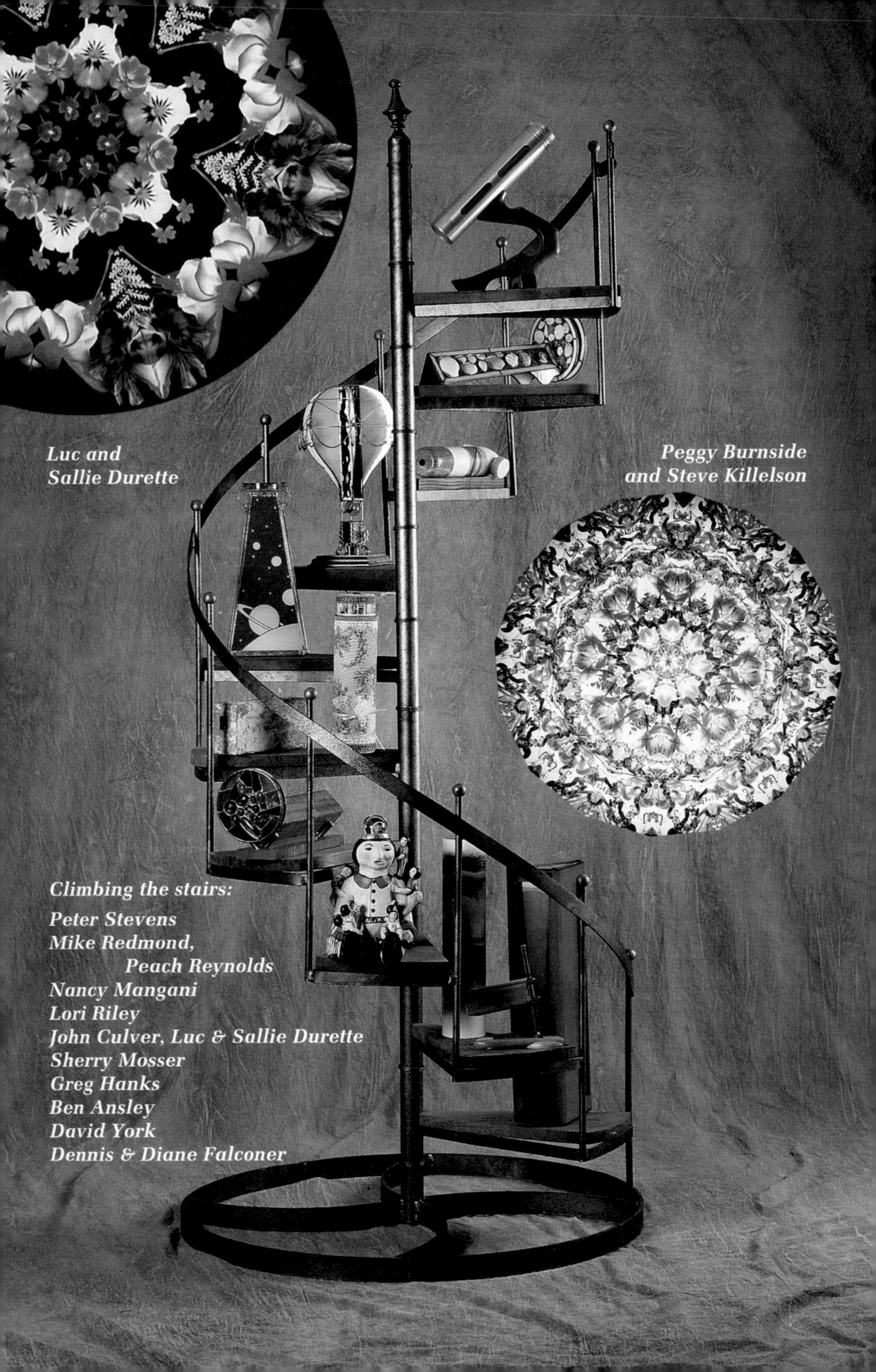

*Luc and
Sallie Durette*

*Peggy Burnside
and Steve Killelson*

Climbing the stairs:

Peter Stevens
Mike Redmond,
        Peach Reynolds
Nancy Mangani
Lori Riley
John Culver, Luc & Sallie Durette
Sherry Mosser
Greg Hanks
Ben Ansley
David York
Dennis & Diane Falconer

vides a more intimate viewing experience and completely immerses the viewer in image, color, and music.

SpectraSphere™ is being produced in a limited edition series of 50 handmade, signed, and numbered projectors. Barbara has also produced, in collaboration with Pat Kehs of Prime Lens Productions, a video which brings the SpectraSphere's unique and colorful kaleidoscopic imagery to the television screen: "A Video of Kaleidoscopic Magic and Enlightenment." Pat Kehs is also working with Barbara in designing large-screen imagery to be used as a dynamic visual element for the performing arts.

Other kaleidoscopes designed by Barbara Mitchell include elaborate one-of-a-kind Pavé Crystal Cosmic Eggs. She also makes an inexpensive plastic version of the Cosmic Egg and, in collaboration with Carolyn Bennett, a "Doodlescope," which allows the viewer to draw his own images.

Christie Moody

Christie Moody loves to experiment and devise different concepts by mixing tried technology with her own artistic expression. The viewing object for her Aquasphere series is a mouthblown sphere, liquid-filled with sparkling pieces. The body of the scope is slumped glass. There is a musical self-turning version, "Music of the Aquasphere," and others in the series include "The Child of Aquasphere," "Journey to the Aquasphere," "Twinstar" (with two separate viewing systems), "Orbit," and "Rain Maker".

Right off the drawing board at Blue Heron Glass Art is a really different kind of scope. The shape of both the body and the object chamber in "Recollections in the Mind's Eye" is different, and even the location of the eyepiece is new. There is nothing to rotate, and when you look through the middle, there is a different image in each direction. (page 180)

Sherry Moser

Sherry Moser is a real innovator. Each scope she introduces contains original ideas and new images. As a kid sitting and painting next to her artist dad, Sherry was convinced that she had not been born with any artistic ability. And since she was sure that was the only way it could be acquired, much as Sherry loved art, she chose nursing as her life's work.

It was while working as a pediatric oncology nurse that Sherry learned to look at the world in a different way. A hospital chaplain, teaching the hospital staff how to reduce stress, influenced Sherry's thinking as he likened each person to a bucket filled with water from which we dip to give of ourselves. He explained that we dip and dip until, if we are not careful, our bucket becomes empty.

The "Sphaera"

"He was trying to teach us to take care of ourselves," Sherry observed, "so that our buckets would not become empty. Kaleidoscopes became my way of refilling my bucket. They brought the tranquility and peace needed to balance a stressful professional life."

Later Sherry combined her two hobbies — kaleidoscopes and stained glass — and discovered she was capable of producing a form of art after all. And one that is not only beautiful to behold — but one in which the very making is an outlet for releasing tension and stress. Sherry soon switched from nursing to kaleidoscoping.

In 1992, Sherry Moser won the Brewster Society Award for Creative Ingenuity for her kaleidoscope, "Journey". Using a totally unique process, the mirrors in this scope become an integral part of the whole image. This represents a remarkable breakthrough in kaleidoscope construction. Other important Moser Kaleidoscopes include PrisMagica, Chandala, Fairie Dreams, Light Dancer, and Sphaera.

"I believe that kaleidoscopes have opened my eyes to an inner self where anything becomes possible," Sherry says, "but Dr. Dale Turner said it best: 'Dreams are renewable. No matter what our age or condition, there are still untapped possibilities within us and new beauty waiting to be born.'"

Craig Musser

Craig Musser, a leading forerunner in the kaleidoscope renaissance, died in September, 1986. His kaleidoscopes will live as a standard of excellence.

While studying Buddhism in India, Craig Musser realized the similarity of kaleidoscope patterns to the Mandala designs used in meditation. He was filled with awe when he first saw a Bush scope. At first he thought the Bush instrument could not be improved upon, but it slowly occurred to him that there had to be optical quality mirrors available in today's market that were not available a hundred years ago. Moreover, by adding sophisticated and intricate glass objects and more imaginative colors, one could transform the kaleidoscope of old into a magnificent modern treasure. In his quest for the best, he set out to find a superior glass blower, and this led him to Bill O'Connor.

Together they produced a limited edition of 50 kaleidoscopes known as Van Dyke Series II. Hailed by an ardent collector as the "Rolls-Royce" of kaleidoscopes and referred to in the Smithsonian Magazine as the "ultimate" kaleidoscope, Series II is no longer available. The price was $3,800 in 1982 and now has more than doubled for any that might become available. The magic and nostalgia of the Victorian Bush scope endure in Series II, but the images have advanced to a zenith of perfection unparalleled. (see title page)

Series III changed direction in style, but not in quality or optics. Stunningly sleek and modern in design, this handsome  instrument rests in its own wooden, oblong, leather-lined stand. It is a limited edition of 350, each signed and numbered. A built-in recessed bronze dial controls the image, presenting an optimum illusion in a minimal space. . . for while the glass pieces are smaller, they are more intricate, and the images are seen behind a hand-faceted glass lens.

The spiritual aspect of the kaleidoscope as well as its magic was meaningful to Craig Musser. "I often experience a renewal of spirit when I look into a kaleidoscope," Craig mused. "From a random jumble of pieces, an infinite number of never-repeating, stunningly beautiful images appear. I am reminded of such basic principles as the ever-changing quality of the universe, the necessity for destruction of the old to generate the new, the complete unpredictability of existence and the underlying order that is inhumanly beautiful."

I can never muse upon the origin
of my interest in kaleidoscopes
without graphically recalling
the indelible impact of Craig Musser's
talent and humanity.

Gary Newlin

Whether tucked between hot dog stands at a country fair or set up along the parade route that leads to a community oyster roast, the Touch of Glass booth is a major attraction. The interest of the crowds that gather is infectious. "I haven't seen one of these since I was a kid," and "How I used to love these," are common exclamations as people stop to admire Gary Newlin's kits.

Gary was the first to package a copper kit containing all of the components needed to assemble a finished scope with instructions easy enough for an eight-year-old to follow and complete in less than an hour.

Before he launched a Touch of Glass, Gary's career was in childhood development, so it was natural to blend his interests and his talents. The results are very rewarding.

Mentally and physically handicapped children are not often accorded a leisure-time activity other than television. "Most of them have never been allowed to do anything like this before," he explains. "When they start seeing the colors and making the kaleidoscopes, they get fired up."

But the real satisfaction comes when the children finish their work. "They get positive feedback," Gary says with enthusiasm. "And that makes them feel good. It gives them increased feelings of worth."

Axel Nilsson

Axel Nilsson Designs is more than just a company, it is a family with a tradition of excellence dating back to Axel Nilsson of Sweden, born in 1873. Today this tradition of old-world craftsmanship and quality is combined with innovative classic design and is carried on by Axel's son, grandson and their families.

The Axel Nilsson family has been making kaleidoscopes by hand for approximately seven years in their workshop located high on a mountain overlooking the beautiful Napa Valley, in the heart of northern California's wine country. They feel the slower pace of this environment gives them more time to pay special attention to the details of their kaleidoscopes.

All of Axel's scopes have the unique feature of an accessible object chamber allowing one to be an artist by adding objects of different shapes and colors to this chamber.

Axel's latest creation is the Cinescope. Two models are available: One that projects an actual turning kaleidoscopic image on a screen self contained within the unit, and another that projects the kaleidoscopic image onto a wall or other surface. A zoom lens is available that, within this latest creation, allows the actual kaleidoscopic image to be projected on a wall in sizes ranging from small to very large. (page 180)

Nityaprema

Magic wands have a universal appeal and intrigue, being a source of wonder throughout the ages. Fashioned from timeless designs, they symbolize ancient tools of wisdom, authority, and magic, and are used today as meaningful aids to meditation and healing, as decorator items, jewelry to wear, and treasures to collect. They bring reality to the rituals of weddings, religious celebrations, birthdays, and other rites of passage.

Nityaprema makes an extraordinary variety of wands, sceptres and flutes, incorporating either a teleidoscope or a kaleidoscope into many of them. The viewer looks through a faceted quartz crystal or through gemstones into a crystal, and this gives an illusion of walking through a crystal cave or forest.

Nitya's wands are made by hand from a high-quality brass that is then heavily plated with gold or silver in an ancient art form process of hand dipping. The metal sculpting is done with a soft silver solder and is not cast, so that every wand has its own design of swirls. Each one contains a jewelry quality quartz crystal on one end and an amethyst crystal on the opposite end. Many are encrusted with additional rare gems and pearls.

"Quartz crystals are a very powerful medium to be working with," Nitya says. "I feel privileged to be a part of creating new-age tools. Magic wands, like kaleidoscopes, are something that was meant to be — everyone should have a magic wand!"

Nitya also thinks everyone should experience a labyrinth journey. Motivated by a desire to re-enchant the earth, she has moved from magic wands to magic circles. Traveling with her handpainted 27-foot labyrinth throughout the country and beyond, Nitya invites other re-enchanters to walk or dance the rainbow labyrinth.

Bill O'Connor

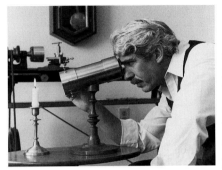

Bill O'Connor is frequently referred to as the Dean of Kaleidoscopists. Until 1988 he had been the only known artist to master the technique of hermetically sealing liquid-filled glass ampules since those patented by Charles Bush in 1870. Bill's are still considered nonpareil as regards shape, color and durability.

Bill first sculpted with wood, but as he sat in his earliest glass-blowing class with Josh Simpson, he knew that he had found his true medium. The "roar of the furnace, the smell of the glass" struck a responsive chord. The process seemed to blend with his personality, and he went about building his own furnaces, which, when completed, produced enough energy to heat his entire house.

Perceiving the moon to be night's mirror, Bill makes his colors run the spectrum from glittering shadows of evening through the faint blush of dawn, bursting into the full radiance of day. Each handblown, lamp-worked tiny glass object is a work of art unto itself, a wee sculpture assuming an exotic shape. There are minarets, shepherds' crooks, horses' manes, lightning bolts, even a unicorn's horn. The finest pieces are hermetically sealed and filled with oils, mica or other tiny colored glass bits to achieve an added dimension of movement. Thirty to forty of these exquisite objects tumble about in the object case, accounting for the dazzlingly spectacular images seen in all of O'Connor's kaleidoscopes, including the Van Dyke series, done in collaboration with the late Craig Musser.

Bill pursues an active interest in archeology and anthropology. Not only does he participate in diggings, he uses man's oldest industry, flint knapping (over two million years old) to add a new gamut to his glass objects.

A love of strong design and pure color comes through each and every piece by Bill O'Connor. Each of the 130 limited-edition Series V brass scopes, as well as the newer ebony and silver version, is signed and numbered, an heirloom to be cherished for generations.

Ralph Olson

"Postcard from Nebraska", narrated by Roger Welsch on CBS Sunday Morning with Charles Kuralt, aired the story of Ralph Olson making kaleidoscopes out of emu and ostrich eggs. Since that time Ralph has received inquiries and orders from Honolulu to Nova Scotia.

To make the eggs into scopes, Ralph inserts a copper kaleidoscope through the length of the eggs. Grace Johnson then paints wildlife and other designs on them. (See page 65) Ralph also makes wooden laser-burned scopes at his Platte River Kaleidoscope Company.

Tom and Carol Paretti

Tom and Carol Paretti's wooden kaleidoscopes are truly professionally hewn, smoothly rubbed, painstakingly polished, and buffed until not a seam in the finish nor a grain of the wood can be felt. "Solid velvet" describes their Workingwood kaleidoscopes.

In 1969, Tom found a kaleidoscope in a Cracker Jack box. He took it apart to see the principle behind the magic. In 1973, he took a design class and made his first kaleidoscope. By 1979, he was selling them, and the rest is part of scope history.

The Parettis make every piece of their scopes with a great deal of care and attention to detail, from the hand-held models in twenty-one different woods to their large special limited editions.

"Efflorescent" is the largest kaleidoscope they have made. It stands 27 inches high and is 20 inches wide and 17 inches deep. The object chamber is 8 1/2 inches in diameter and the magnified image is an unusual flowering conical shape.

Crystal Chameleon is a new touch-activated scope created by Tom and Carol Paretti. While Liquid Crystal is not a new material (it was discovered in Austria in 1888), its visual application to kaleidoscopes is probably the most current idea reviewed in this book. Being liquid and crystal at the same time, the substance flows, yet has the ability to diffract light. Brilliant colors change at the slightest pressure and heat from the fingers.

Both Tom and Carol are especially gratified when they learn that a teacher is using their scopes in a classroom, or that a doctor purchases one for waiting-room relaxation. But they are really happy when they witness an adult's excitement as he peeks through a scope for the first time since childhood.

Steve and David Parman

Parman Brothers, Steve and David, had been making fine wooden furniture for several years before they turned their talents to kaleidoscopes in 1984. They enjoy and take pride in their work and have been successful in their determination to fashion premier quality scopes with very affordable price tags.

Red oak, black walnut and imbuia are the popular hard-woods used in their turning-end scopes. A new line of mini-scopes (7" to 8-1/2") is crafted of beech, with multi-colored inlays.

The Parman brothers agree that "One of the most enjoyable aspects of our involvement with kaleidoscopes has been the opportunity to meet and know other kaleidoscope makers."

Tom Proctor

Tom Proctor makes a smooth ceramic scope with bright acrylic wheels. "Just as mother Earth is a sphere in constant change, so is the kaleidoscope," says Tom Proctor. "With every new turn there is a new discovery."

Since earning a Master's degree in Art at Colorado State in 1956, Tom has been teaching art in the public school system. He initiated a kaleidoscope project for his classes to show his students the infinite possibilities of color and light. His personal interest carried him beyond the experimental cardboard tube variety created in class and ultimately led to lovely porcelain scopes.

Despite his attraction to stained glass, Tom wanted to make a different scope from any he had seen. Intrigued by the delicate flesh tones of the porcelain used by his wife Patricia in making dolls, Tom selected three soft pastel shades for the triangular viewing tubes. Then, in marked contrast, he achieved an unfamiliar look by adding sparkling abstract designs on jewel-toned acrylic wheels. The spin of the wheels is as smooth as the glaze on Tom's porcelain scopes.

Employing his first love, sculpture, Tom has designed and made a handsome piece of bronze sculpture which in no way resembles a scope, but does in fact house a stunning kaleidoscope. (see page 154)

The flowing lines of a feathered bird encircle a small bronze cylinder resting on a base of hand-turned walnut. The eye of the bird is a fine-quality cubic zirconia mounted in 14K gold. This brilliant stone is the only clue to the sparkling visuals to be viewed within its gently tapered structural form.

Tom Raredon

Tom Raredon comes to the world of kaleidoscopes from a background in metallurgical engineering and an abiding interest in functional design. His approach to metal as a versatile and plastic material with a life and a strength of its own is clearly realized in his thoughtful and finely wrought objects which include jewelry, belt buckles, copper cookware, candlesticks and lamps as well as kaleidoscopes.

The American Parlor Kaleidoscope was initially born of a partnership between Stephen Auger and Tom Raredon. Together they created the first series of 100 kaleidoscopes in 1984 which was completely sold out by the end of the following year. The second series, an edition of 350 introduced in

November, 1985, is produced by Tom Raredon Metalwork.

The second series is an even more polished instrument than the kaleidoscope of the first series. The mirror system has been improved using untinted, finely coated first surface mirrors which offer a high degree of reflectivity and ultimately a clearer, crisper image. The objects, still made by Stephen Auger, have become more selective and more refined.

Gordon and Anneliese Redmond

Gordon and Anneliese Redmond make a large variety of both brass and stained glass kaleidoscopes. They are probably best known for Gordon's unique six- and eight-star mirror configuration and Anneliese's elaborately decorated stained glass scopes.

The Redmonds were married in a castle just down the street from where Anneliese lived in Giessen, Germany. Her European background and expertise with traditional stained-glass artwork were influential in developing the idea for the Kaleido-Kastle. (page 71)

Each turret of the castle is a separate scope. One contains a six-mirror version of Gordon's distinctive "star-eight" design. A drawbridge opens to reveal interchangeable wheels, and a music box plays "Camelot."

Another dramatic piece from Old World glass is a large brass floor-model lamp-like scope. Each interchangeable eight inch wheel is individually set with semiprecious stones, dichroic glass, antique beads and cut-glass crystals.

Peach Reynolds
Mark Reynolds

"A kaleidoscope is a lot like life," says Cary Peach Reynolds, one of the first well-known names in the kaleidoworld, "it offers beauty, fantasy, stillness, motion, surprise. It suggests planning and order; it is random and unpredictable."

Peach Reynolds is responsible for a very exciting development — the world's first electronic kaleidoscope. This battery-operated high-tech "electrascope" is activated by sound. By simply pointing it in the direction of any sound source, you can see a miniature display of fireworks. Try some marching-band music or Beethoven's Fifth Symphony and watch those flashing L.E.D.s really jump.

He was also among the first to use front-surfaced, optical-quality mirrors in all of his scopes, assuring crisper, crystal clear images with every turn. "It has at last become an art form accepted by the art establishment," he asserts happily, "so now there is a lot of room for development."

In 1989 Peach stopped making scopes and turned the entire business over to his brother and partner, Mark. In addition to the already large line of scopes, Kaleidovisions continues to expand on the ideas of blending classic designs with innovative applications.

They produce several basic models but the changing pattern of form, color, texture and light brought about by paper clips, comb teeth, sea shells, jewelry, filigree, mardigras beads, stained glass, buttons, sequins and colored oils makes each one individual and exciting. Their "see-through" turns the world into a kaleidoscope. Oil suspension models are made with either colored objects or a variety of tiny sea shells drifting in clear oil. They make a camerascope which screws onto any camera, allowing one to capture on film a kaleidoscope scene of one's choice. The large tubular bodies of a great many of Reynolds's scopes are hand painted with swirls of color, making them easy to recognize. He also makes some with exotic natural woods.

For the overwhelmed and indecisive, there is a handsome darkwood partitioned case which holds one kaleidoscope with six interchangeable end pieces. Or, if someone wants a more personalized scope, Kaleidovisions will create a personal one in which the customer's favorite trinkets and treasures — say a petal from an old corsage or a baby's tooth — can be forever immortalized.

Lori Riley

Kaleidoscopes were a natural for Lori Riley. Her mother is Janice Chesnik and her sister is Sheryl Koch. Lori had been making and selling scopes in Hawaii for a couple of years before moving to the mainland. She makes several models, some using Hawaiian koa wood, but her unique variation of the two-mirror system produces an image that appears quite different. There is no outline of a circle, no surrounding background — just a dramatic star suspended in space.

Ward Robison

"No less than his creations, Ward Robison is a study in contrasts . . . Ex-trucker, animal lover, musician, devotee of the science of blackjack as much as of the thrill of gambling, trained glass-beveler, bon-vivant and a man who can declare passionately, 'It doesn't matter,' while even more passionately devoting himself to proving it does, conservator and innovator, technician and artist: one whose vision naturally encompasses the shifting light of life reflected by fixed planes: a born kaleidoscope maker." (This profile is from an article by Paul Mallory.)

In Ward Robison's words: "A friend who teaches math recently pointed out that my two major diversions were both based on mathematics. Kaleidoscopes of course are based on geometry. The other passion he was referring to is my enthusiasm for casino blackjack. A serious effort at the game requires an understanding of the mathematics of probabilities. By the way, I found it easier to gather an extensive library of books on the subject of blackjack than to gather a few pages of technical information on kaleidoscopes."

In 1989 Ward collaborated with renowned painter and sculptor, Tom Palmerton, to produce "Seen in the Wood." They planned for this bronze sculpture scope to be a limited edition of 25. However, a tragic fire destroyed Tom Palmerton's entire lifetime of work, including the mold for "Seen in the Wood." Only three models exist. A concealed rotatable object cell contains, among other items, ampules with bi-colored oils. The two-mirror system produces a nine-point image.

Both a two-mirror (20-fold symmetry) and a three-mirror system that contains three types of symmetry are housed in Ward's latest mode, "Quartet," crafted in collaboration with Tom Seidel. Options for viewing also include both stained-glass wheels and object cells that contain free-falling pieces which can be added to and removed, as well as interchanged.

The wheels and cell are the same diameter as the tube and turn on a central axis. The crystal barrels with brass end pieces are lined with brocade which is available in different colors or the collector can provide his own fabric. A matching brass stand completes an elegant presentation.

David and Marty Roenigk

Sir David's Reflections was started by brothers David and Marty Roenigk. Marty had been collecting and selling antique scopes for years. David repaired and restored them. As the originals became harder to find and the prices continued to soar, the Roenigks decided to produce an authentic reproduction of the Bush scope. Exact in every detail, it was unveiled at the 1989 Strathmore Exhibition.

The Queen Anne and Victoria II are among a few additional old models that David and Marty reproduced. They employed Stephen Auger to design some special objects to give the old styles an updated image.

David Rosenfeldt
Debbie Brodel

"We are Shipwrecked!" is the recorded message and business name for Debbie Brodel and David Rosenfeldt. Determined to come up with something new that could make their work readily recognizable, they designed a different shape wheel. Each flower wheel is made of many glass petals which are lovingly cut and shaped to produce a blossom. (page 65)

Tiny blown glass figures, randomly attached, add interest and tend to scatter and compound the image. Their new colossal models (one is musical) contain a bi-optical mirror system, and have three wheels, each on its own axle.

Sue Ross

Sue Ross made her first scope while in Brownies at age seven. And like many scope makers, the first scope she made to sell was a simple stained-glass triangular body with a marble as the viewing object. She started decorating the marble scopes with ornate trimmings, then made wheel scopes with elaborate embellishments.

To date, she has made a variety of stained glass scopes. Most noteworthy are a reproduction of an old French toy scope (Dépose Kaleidopik II) and a Carousel Lamp Scope, a two piece scope which illuminates. The Carousel is made with three separate themes: Metamorphosis of a Butterfly, Neon Irides (Rainbow) and Orb Weaver Spider.

Sue feels that the longevity of the kaleidoscope is everlasting, and says, "I am convinced that the children of present collectors will hand this interest down to their children or grandchildren. I would like to see the kaleidoscope remain in a design that is easily recognizable as a kaleidoscope and not of a design that causes one to wonder what it is."

Shantidevi

Shantidevi's work is about healing. In her own words, "It's about bringing some light, laughter, and natural order into a world that has lost its connection to a natural sense of the divine."

Glass has been Shanti's passion since 1978. Working with it professionally since then, she has pushed beyond design limitations, innovated many new techniques, and won awards for her delicate and rare solder sculpture.

Kaimana Art Glass originated in Hawaii in 1982 with the partnership of Shantidevi and **Ritama.** "Kaimana" is ancient Hawaiian meaning "sparkling light dancing on the waves, joyously reflecting the ocean's inherent power." That wording aptly describes the kaleidoscopes handcrafted by Shanti and Ritama. They retained the flavor of Hawaii even after they moved to California as they continued to fuse sea shells and crystals into elaborate silver soldering. (page 179) In 1988 Shanti and Ritama began working separately. Shanti kept the name Kaimana Art Glass and Ritama's scopes are known as the Valhalla Collection.

Shanti set up a hot glass studio focusing on solid spheres of glass filled with "glittering landscapes of the spirit." **Sugito,** a longtime friend, started working with Shanti. He designed and created the "Healing Lights" series originally for an AIDS benefit art auction. He also collaborated in the design and execution of "Let the Dreamers Wake the Nation" (page 70) and the "Pyramuse."

Shanti's scopes range in size from tiny pendants to large sculptured pieces with spheres up to five inches in diameter. Whatever Shanti sets out to do, she accomplishes with flying colors. Her newest pieces are different from anything she has done before. The bodies are glass with bas relief sculpture done in clay, then painted with dichroic acrylic paints. The objects are her own blown spheres.

It is Shanti's hope that her work will "move one, if even for a moment, to a place that is bigger than all of us and contains all of our differences in grace and beauty, a reminder of our unity with all."

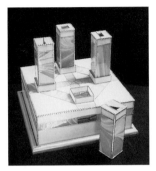

Kerry Shepherd

For several years Kerry Shepherd made a variety of stained-glass scopes. Before changing careers, Kerry designed the Party Scope. An inner light shines through two 15" bejeweled wheels. Four separate scopes rest on clear glass windows which permit views into the backlit wheels. Each viewer sees an entirely different image as each scope is built with a different optical system.

Peter Stephens

One of the most innovative ultramodern kaleidoscopes is the Phase-Turbine™, by optical artist Peter Stephens. For several years Peter worked at San Francisco's Exploratorium, doing maintenance and redesign on other people's inventions. Then he designed his own portable "light show," shedding new light on an old vision.

This sleek scope introduced two new features: an internal light source and a revolutionary image-generating means. It is constructed of instrument-grade brass with areas of aluminum finished in black crackle. An internal light source allows the image maximum color saturation and infinite reflective image multiplication.

Three wheels are designed to spin rapidly and for extended periods of time when flicked into motion by the viewer. Each wheel has a different specific function: one provides color, one provides a basic pattern, and one, called a slit scanner, breaks the basic pattern down into a series of moving dots which move about so rapidly that the eye and brain retain a summation of the cyclic motion of the dots to create the image. All three wheels in motion visually interfere with one another and enter into phase relationships resulting in a constantly transforming cyclic image of form and color. (Eight interchangeable pattern disks are included.)

Peter designed an oil filled acrylic scope, Tunnel of Light, before licensing his patent and moving into other areas of optics.

Willie Stevenson

Kaleidoscope making for Willie Stevenson was an accidental, but very natural, combination of his blacksmithing and glassworking skills. He lives in a small mountain town in North Carolina that time has passed by. Having given up a traditional life style to pursue the Guiding Light, Willie named the enterprise, "Spirit Scopes."

Willie was the first to introduce an affordable, two-mirror, handheld scope. Prior to that time, very few scopes, other than expensive table models, contained the two-mirror system. This started a new trend, and today there are as many, or more, two-mirror scopes of every type. Spirit Scopes are meticulously crafted of copper and no two are exactly alike. Each is a striking piece of flame-oxidized sculpture. To the newest "Landscape" series, a brilliant turquoise color has been added.

To the extent that we know, from the time Brewster patented his polyangular scope in 1820, no one had designed a similar instrument until Willie Stevenson came out with the "Alpha" in 1988. Before the end of the decade, a few other artists were experimenting with polyangular pieces, and Spirit

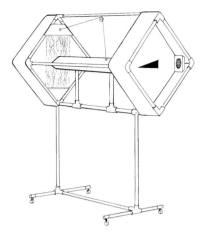

Scopes had created other models, including Home Planet. (page 116)

Willie's most notable piece to date, "Whatever Blows Your Skirt Up" or (to add a touch of Scottish brogue) "Whatever Tilts Your Kilt," won the Brewster Society Award for Creative Ingenuity in 1989.

It is a large, motorized, polyangular floor- model kaleidoscope (6'L x 6'H x 3'W). The object box contains handpainted silk scarves blowing above a fan. At the flip of a switch, the 12" x 48" mirrors automatically open and close, revealing stunning six- to fifteen-point imagery. These randomly formed images move in perfect rhythm with music emanating from stereo speakers located on either side of the eyepiece.

"Silk Dancer" is a smaller, vertical version of "Whatever Blows Your Skirt Up" in a limited edition of 25. It is a free-standing floor model made of black and colored Lucite, measuring 16" square by 44" tall. Completely automatic, it features continuously variable polyangular mirrors with internal and external silks hand painted by Willie, and music that is "cerebrally synchronized" so that the images "dance," hence the name. (page 181)

Glenn and Ben Straub

Designing more in the style of traditional kaleidoscopes, Glenn and Ben Straub seem to embody the best of the Pennsylvania Dutch countryside where they reside: serenity, simplicity, and naturalness. Their business, Wood You Believe, came about via toolmaking and

woodworking (inlaid vases, bowls, and jewelry) and evolved into kaleidoscopes, which now occupy almost all of their time.

Glenn and Ben produce both a series of classic pedestal models and streamlined, hand-held styles. All the scopes are made of exotic woods which are lovingly culled from six continents. Each piece of cathedral glass used in the object cases is flame-sculpted. Antique watch parts add a textured pattern to the images, seen sharp and clear through fine first-surface mirrors.

The Signature Edition and Recollection Series Parlour Kaleidoscopes are made in a limited edition, signed, numbered, and dated. Standing approximately 14" high, they are available in American black walnut or white ash. A clever and convenient feature differentiates the SF (sculptural form) one-of-a-kind series: the barrel lifts out of the pedestal for easy viewing. Handsome hand-held models are available in a wide variety of woods: mahogany, walnut, bird's eye maple, rosewood, zebrano, padauk, and elm burl.

The Straubs are among the few who have mastered the technique of making handblown liquid-filled ampules, which are included in the object cells of the higher-end Wood You Believe scopes. And, without a doubt, the very top of their line is "Kaleiope," a magnificent, jumbo wooden parlor scope. (page 180) It contains two separate mirror systems: one producing a 3-D sphere, and a completely new optical system that creates a rectangular carousel effect, hard to describe, but eye-boggling to view!

"We don't use stains or dyes," Glenn says, "but prefer to let the woods speak for themselves" — something they do quite eloquently. Purple-heart from South America gives off a fine amethyst gleam, while ceylonese satinwood glows like spun gold.

Burlwood is another favorite with the intricate design of the wood forming a mandala-like pattern to complement the scope's mandala interior. In fact, mandalas have long interested Glenn as a way of meditating and centering today's frenetic lifestyle while bringing into focus the harmony and synchronization of colors that all too often seem absent.

"The optical symmetry of the mandala helps man to emerge from a closely personal experience in order to reach a comprehensive view of the universal and enables that viewer to expand beyond himself."

Daniel Tarr

Daniel Tarr sees light and color as "a key to meaning behind the veil and therapy for body and soul." Each one of us sees different colors as shades of perception," Dan explains. "With the kaleidoscope as our universe, we become the Architect — imposing order out of chaos, changing emotions, and realizing the harmony of diversity."

Reminiscent of the old stereoscopic viewers, Dan makes a distinctive stained-glass StereoScope which is actually a pair of binoculars with three, four, and even five mirrors. It fits right up around the eyes and produces a strong dimensional effect. Two removable and asymmetrical color wheels are employed  which are made of many pieces of etched, textured, dichroic, antique, iridescent, European, and domestic mouthblown and hand-rolled glass. In some of the scopes, Dan inserts a piece of curled film for a special "swirl" variation.

Dan would like to be able to make a recording of the involuntary verbal response such as ooooh, ahhhh and wow that he hears when people look through these scopes. Meanwhile, he urges folks to "try one on for sighs!"

Mike and Linda Thurston

To the customer's question, "What's new?", Mike and Linda Thurston (Gemini Kaleidoscopes) always have a ready answer, since they produce several new scopes each year.

It's important to the Thurstons to make scopes that youngsters can afford with camera-grade optics that their parents can enjoy. They also provide a wide range of activity kits that allow the children to learn the mechanics of a scope while enjoying the pleasures of creating their own kaleidoscope art.

Since 1983 Gemini has been turning out good quality cardboard scopes in the low price range. Using materials made only in the USA, Gemini successfully combines handcraft work with mass production and ships hundreds of thousands all over the world.

Toby Tobecksen

Tobar Designs is a combination of Toby Tobecksen and his wife Barbara's first names. They make affordable carousel musical wood-and-glass kaleidoscopes. Whether bejeweled, painted, or decorated with pressed flowers, no two carousels are alike, and more than fifty music box tunes are available.

Some carousels are made entirely of crystals, while others are theme oriented with motifs such as art deco, Native American, Southwest, or personally customized. Toby takes great pride in his workmanship.

Erik and Kate Van Cort

Van Cort Instruments, Inc. probably makes more fine precision-tooled instruments than any other maker. Past and present converge convincingly in the Van Cort kaleidoscopes. These artful instruments of the past are put together with the technology of today's precision tool making. Neither art nor nostalgia was responsible for the beginning of Van Cort Instruments, however. Rather, it was a keen business sense coupled with basic know-how that moved the Van Corts into the field.

Erik and Kate Van Cort began their business in 1979, when they sold the large floor-tripod telescopes they built. These were accurate reproductions of telescopes originally used in Countinghouses in the 1800's to spot pennant flags on incoming clipper ships. By 1982, they had reproduced an orrery from the Smithsonian Collection and telescopes, one from the

Colonial Williamsburg Foundation and the other from Monticello. In addition, they reproduced a working sundial.

In 1983, they made their first kaleidoscope, the Lucida, similar in design to production kaleidoscopes made during the first kaleidoscope bonanza, around 1820-1830. Next was a very elaborate reproduction of an early desk-top kaleidoscope made by English instrument makers around 1825. They appropriately called it the Classic.

Kaleidoscopes of all sorts of designs and new devices occupied them through 1987, when they outgrew their studio in Holyoke, Massachusetts. In 1988, they moved into their new, state-of-the-art workshop in Northampton, Massachusetts, with the Dragonfly™, a multifaceted optical device, consuming all of their energies. By 1989, they completed the plans they had worked on for years, and reproduced what Eric refers to as "probably the greatest production kaleidoscope that ever existed, the Charles G. Bush™ kaleidoscope."

Regarding their future plans, Erik and Kate are reaching beyond kaleidoscopes and telescopes and searching into the past to recreate the beauty that once was. Their offering of reproductions of scientific instruments, with a blend of some of their own contemporary designs, will occupy the next few years for Kate and Erik Van Cort.

Lesley Wadsworth

Lesley Wadsworth was one of the first kaleidoscopists to make two-wheel scopes (1977), and the very first, to my knowledge, to use dichroic glass in both the wheels and body of the kaleidoscope. She was also the first to make scopes using the Jearl Walker mirror arrangement referred to in the January, 1986 *Scientific American*. It has since been established that a few artists, including Stephen Auger and Charles Karadimos, were already using the configuration of 30-60-90, but only a very few were using other than an equilateral triangle prior to Walker's article. Lesley thinks this formula represents the most beautiful design of all the three-mirror systems because it offers three types of symmetry, the maximum in any unambiguous image field.

Lesley makes one of the few scopes that are even more astonishing when viewed with artificial light than with sunlight. The wheels are made with over forty different colors of dichroic glass, portions of it etched, slumped, textured, and multicolored. The barrel is covered with Ultrasuede cloth with cutouts that richly enhance the image.

Kirk Webber

You can almost taste the colors as the hot glass wheels spin on Kirk Webber's kaleidoscopes. And you can feel the silken grain in the barrels of both his handheld and pedestal scopes, fashioned from exotic woods such as aspen, Indian rosewood, padauk, cherry, walnut, and oak. Some are patterned with interesting inlays.

Kirk was one of the first to use real flowers in his wheels. A special 24-hour drying process is used that leaves the brilliant colors intact; this enhances the imagery. But Kirk is the first to admit that while he enjoys the images inside kaleidoscopes, it is the patterns and textures of the wood he uses that are the real fascination for him.

Corki Weeks

Corki Weeks was the first recipient of the Brewster Society Award for Creative Ingenuity. Her idea in 1986 to build two separate mirror systems into one kaleidoscope body initiated a major step forward in the scope industry.

As a fiber artist and stained-glass craftsman for many years prior to designing kaleidoscopes, Corki first focused her attention on the scope's exteriors. After experimenting with the optics and objects inside, however, Corki turned her attention to the interior workings.

Although Corki insists that "simplicity is always best," she makes a large line of brass scopes, ranging from pendants to pedestals, which include some very sophisticated and complex styles. She has started using the durable, marblelike Corian for some sleek new models and, in that medium, has created two large parlour scopes that stand twelve to fifteen inches tall, with shapes and curves reminiscent of the art deco era.

Looking back, Corki concedes, "The best part of the scope scene has been the friendships and helping hands I've found along the way. My staff makes keeping up with the pace possible. Without them there would be no Corki Weeks Kaleidoscopes."

Danny Wilson

What differentiates Danny Wilson's scopes from others is his unique dual-axis rotating object wheel. This squirrel-cage spinner wheel can be turned on one axis to change the colors and when the other axis is turned, the designs change.

The Spinner is built by means of stained-glass techniques and extensive solder-sculpting. The three-inch spinner wheel contains a rainbow of colors, textures, dichroic glass, jewels, and solder designs — attractive to look at as well as into.

The Polaris is a marble scope with a four-mirror system which creates dual-centered, counter-rotating imagery. For the viewing object, Danny uses a 1-1/2" handblown marble by Shantidevi, which is attached to the scope by solder sculpted claws and a removable spring wire.

Kay Winkler

Kay Winkler specializes in 15° two-mirror kaleidoscopes made of stained glass. This mirror configuration gives a multifaceted 12-point image that resembles a rose window.

In collaboration with china painter Cassie Marceron, Kay has developed a series of handpainted scopes featuring violets or roses. After painting, the glass is fired in a kiln, and the design becomes permanent. Each scope is one-of-a-kind.

In the object case, Kay uses a large assortment of antique glass beads, flameworked threads, twists, and dichroic glass. Each of the many pieces is carefully chosen with an eye to color and balance to enhance the beauty of the random patterns.

"Working with kaleidoscopes is really rewarding and relaxing," Kay says. "I find them therapeutic as well as inspirational. Taking the time to enjoy the calming effect of the patterns can relieve tensions and also renew, rejuvenate, and reactivate the creative process."

Marshall Yeager

A person steps into his own world of vision in a kaleidoscope. The experience is personal. Only the viewer is seeing and feeling this mystical phenomenon. Part of the charm and intrigue is in this very privacy. It's almost as though it holds magic secrets for the viewer alone.

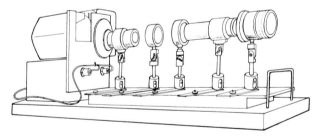

I was afraid projecting the images onto a screen and sharing the experience with others would diminish the impact of "splendid isolation." So it was with great trepidation that I viewed (in 1984) the Kaleidoplex, the first projection kaleidoscope of any significance. My fears were unfounded. The experience was uplifting, exhilarating, eye-boggling — in fact, I could exhaust all my magnificent superlatives and still be at a loss for words!

Synchronized dancing patterns come and go, and go to come again. "It's all done with mirrors," says Kaleidoplex's inventor, Marshall Yeager. "The light-projection device is based on the principle of the kaleidoscope," he explains. Quite simply, the Kaleidoplex creates colored imagery to sound.

The prototype, built from Yeager's designs, was developed by Walter Reiche of East Coast Camera, Inc. Reiche's machine (which never went into production) is an impressive red-and-black assemblage of mirrors, lenses, motors, and aluminum almost three feet long, 14 inches high, and weighing 65 pounds.

Marshall became interested in the kinetic art form of lights while he was co-producer of the sound and light spectacular, "Heavy Organ," starring Virgil Fox, which premiered in New York City in the 70s and toured for many years.

As a result of this involvement, Marshall did research and experimented until he discovered an optical principle that allowed him to send a projected kaleidoscopic image into a second kaleidoscope projection. This method was the basis for Yeager's patent.

David York

From the first day David York visited a kaleidoscope show at Flowers Just Because in California and met some of the Brewster Society family, he became a full-time kaleidoscopist. "I instantly knew that this was for me," David declares. That was in 1987 and he is still making scopes.

The open spaces of New Mexico, along the banks of the Rio Chama, provide the perfect place for David to combine his interest in stained glass work with his life-long fascination with astronomy. Here he spends his days making kaleidoscopes and his nights observing stars.

As a member of the AAVO (American Association of Variable-Star Observers), David is one of the top five observers and is shooting for the number one spot. It takes 20,000 observations for the honor of being the best. This dedicated group, in addition to making visual brightness estimates of variable stars, acts as "advance scouts" for the space program.

"Moon and Stars" is the name of the most popular scope that David makes. It is an 18" triangular tube of stained glass embellished with lunar and stellar designs, and it uses two interchangeable wheels with fused glass nuggets, sea shells, agates and other translucent pieces of glass. Viewing accessories include extra wheels, a stand, and a small light to shine through the rainbow.

While peering behind yesterday,
through the tiny peep-hole of a kaleidoscope,
one can almost glimpse beyond tomorrow.

Scope-Related Art and Artists

IRENE HOLLER

Separate bits and pieces interweave,

Creating spontaneous change.

Then, the wondrous variations intensify,

Manifesting illimitable optical illusions

— A world of euphoric echoes

Scope-Related Art and Artists

The kaleidoscope has become synonymous with mandalic imagery and with anything involving rapid change, variation of colors and patterns, or even the thrill of the unexpected. Sir David Brewster declared in his original patent that:

> The kaleidoscope (from χαλos, beautiful; ∈ισs, a form; and οχοπ∈ω, to see) is an instrument for creating and exhibiting an infinite variety of beautiful forms, and is constructed in such a manner as either to please the eye by an ever-varying succession of splendid tints and symmetrical forms, or to enable the observer to render permanent such as may appear most appropriate for any of the numerous branches of the ornamental arts.

> ...It would be an endless task to point out the various purposes in the ornamental arts to which the kaleidoscope is applicable. It may be sufficient to state, that it will be of great use for architects, ornamental painters, plasterers, jewellers, carvers and gliders, cabinet makers, wire workers, bookbinders, calico printers, carpet manufacturers, manufacturers of pottery, and every other profession in which ornamental patterns are required."

> The painter may introduce the very colours which he is to use; the jeweler, the jewels which he is to arrange; and in general, the artist may apply to the instrument the materials which he is to embody, and thus form the most correct opinion of their effect when combined into an ornamental pattern. When the instrument is thus applied, an infinity of patterns are created, and the artist can select such as he considers most suitable to his work.

Many artists, in fact, do render permanent symmetrical forms that are appropriate for their type of art.

Irene Holler

Irene Holler is a believer in divine order, whether it be in the universe or artistic designs. Painting objects and scenes in repeated segments which radiate from the center, Irene translates kaleidoscopic pictures onto canvas. She calls them "colorscopes."

As a child, Irene was frustrated by the fact that a treasured view in a kaleidoscope would vanish with just a tiny movement of the wrist, never to return. She found a way to have her view and keep it too. Using watercolors, ink, colored pencils, acrylics or egg tempera as well as oils, Irene converts figures and fantasies, by way of pigments and brush, into emotionally charged mandalas.

Joyously enthusiastic about her own creations, Irene says, "My colorscopic designs almost paint themselves and they seem to take on a life of their own."

Ray Howlett

The ideas of Ray Howlett, an optical technician in space light sculpture, encompass a precise, skillful combination of etched and dichroic-coated glass shapes that are lighted from within. The light images are repeatedly reflected inward and turn into a vast array of color. There seems to be space where there is no space.

Ray is experimenting with

sculptures that really are transparent kaleidoscopes — a total-environment scope. As a person looks inside, everything in the room is visible; viewed at a distance, it is all color, because the sides and ends are transparent and yet highly reflective.

Ray describes his work as "a viewer participation art form that to some may inspire meditation."

Paula Nadelstern

Paula Nadelstern makes quilts on the block in the Bronx where she grew up. The tiny quilt-making spaces in her family's apartment have shaped the direction of her quilt art, causing her to rely on intricate detail and inherent symmetry. Paula is intrigued by the structure of fabricated kaleidoscopes, and by the mechanical skill involved in the intricate piecework combined with the challenge of finding the relationships between fabrics. Ten pieces comprise her "Kaleidoscopic" series.

Paula's quilts have been showcased on ABC, CBS, and PBS, as well as in numerous books, including two she has authored: *"Quilting Together"* and *"Color Design in Patchwork."* She has been a Quilt Artist in Residence in New York City Public Schools and winner of many national contests.

"I am personally delighted by quilts which lead the audience toward a multilayered point of view," Paula explains. "My ambition is to harmoniously integrate the 'idea' of a kaleidoscope with the techniques and materials of quiltmaking. In *Kaleidoscopic V: 'The Turning Point,'* I tried to create the illusion of a multifaceted, multifractured surface illuminated by backlighting. A turning point is defined as a point in time at which a decisive change occurs. This refers specifically and metaphorically to the kaleidoscope imagery."

She walks in beauty, like the night
    Of cloudless climes and starry skies;
And all that's best of dark and bright
    Meet in her aspect and her eyes:
Thus mellow'd to that tender light
    Which heaven to gaudy day denies.

—Byron

"Lord Byron"
by
Carmen and Stephen Colley

Images from kaleidoscopes by Judith Karelitz

(From left rear) Carolyn Bennett, Sam Douglas (four), Judith Karelitz, (middle) Dean Kent, Audrey Barna (egg), (front center) Denise Jones

"Pipe Dream" by Adam Peiperl

"Efflorescent" by Tom and Carol Paretti

Wiley Jobe's polyangular floor-model kaleidoscope

"The Jedburgh" by Larry Christensen

156

"Aurora" by Luc and Sallie Durette
*Fresh flowers create
seasonal images*

"Fantasy" by Corki Weeks

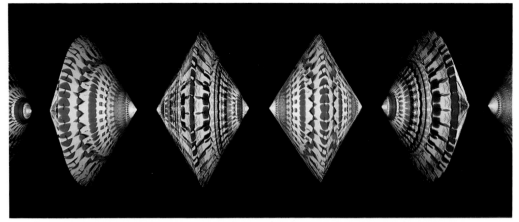

"Parasol" image by Steven Gray

Doug Johnson

Gray & Gray Woodwrights

*Interior polarized designs
by Adam Peiperl
through kaleidoscopes by
Charles Karadimos
and Glenn Straub*

Adam Peiperl

Kinetic artist Adam Peiperl was working with the changing spectral colors of polarized light long before he became interested in kaleidoscopes. Over the past two decades his sculptures utilizing light have been shown across the country, including a 20-year exhibit at the Smithsonian's National Museum of American History.

After visiting a kaleidoscope exhibition at Strathmore Hall Arts Center, Adam started experimenting with new and various ways of incorporating the birefringent material he employs in his sculptures into the object cells for kaleidoscopes.

Although polarized light has been associated with kaleidoscopes since its discovery by Brewster in 1816, until recently very few artists have worked with such materials. Certainly no one has achieved such startling effects as those produced by Adam Peiperl.

Not content to make cells for the SpectraSphere and for other artists' scopes, Adam designed and built a large kaleidoscope sculpture of his own, securing a patent for its method in December, 1992. The Pipe Dream and Bengal Light can best be described as sleekly modern space-age spectaculars.

Adam also excels in photography. He has devised a photographic process that synthesizes a vivid 3-D image from a flat kaleidoscope interior. His interior images have been published on the covers of several college textbooks and journals, and adorn several pages of this book. He has also taken the first interior photographs (to my knowledge) through an original Brewster polyangular kaleidoscope (page 16).

R. Charles Ringsmuth

R. Charles Ringsmuth's research has taken him into the ethereal beauty of the mandala and thus kaleidoscopes. He has evolved his own idiom of kaleidoscopic art which he calls "Cyclicollage". For over 20 years, Charles has been researching the illusion of cyclic movement on a two-dimensional surface.

The Cyclicollage process involves creating an illusion of movement in space via a repetition and variation of graphic images weaving in and out of an equilateral triangular matrix. The medium, paper and acrylic on canvas, lends itself to a variety of visual expressions.

Ringsmuth has been invited to exhibit his large pieces in galleries from Paris to New York to California. He has taught two- and three-dimensional design, and several of his "transpersonal" art pieces have won awards.

Robert Stephan

Robert Stephan is endeavoring to bring a fresh new style of design into the glass medium by using internal colors and air inclusions in his designs. "The real challenge," Robert says, "is to successfully combine the varying factors of blown glass, transparency, light and color all into one finished piece."

Robert taught himself the fundamentals of hot glass and fabricated his first furnace from a fifty-five gallon steel drum. Never satisfied to let his glass pieces remain the same, in 1987 Bob designed the first blown art-glass kaleidoscope.

His newest creation, "Art-tech Dichro-Sphere," employs the pure form of a sphere as the exterior with a dichroic sculpture suspended within. Not surprisingly, Bob engineered the tools necessary for the sphere's fine finish, as well as the equipment for applying dichroic optical coatings to sculptural glass forms.

Each scope-related sculpture is a statement of the artist's "joy in creation and the beauty inherent in God's world."

Betty Tribe

Betty Tribe's kaleidoscopic drawings evolved quite by accident, not from a particular love of kaleidoscopes. However, Betty now admits that she has become an ardent scope enthusiast, fascinated not only with kaleidoscopes, but with the kindred kaleido-spirit of the people involved, be it designer, shop owner, or collector.

It was for a fine arts thesis project that Betty combined her keen interests in texture, symmetry, balance, and intricate mirror image into a precision pencil drawing of her favorite subjects. The response of everyone was, "Oh, they look like kaleidoscopes!" Thus, transforming the familiar, such as that found in nature and fantasy into the unique with colored pencil drawings became her specialty. Betty designs note cards as well as various-size wall hangings.

Woven throughout the years has also been a spiritual quest that has taken Betty along many paths. "It has often seemed to me that growing in truth is like playing `crack the whip'... sometimes we are at the end of the line that is nearly catapulted into oblivion... sometimes we are the anchor person who gives momentum to others... and other times we are somewhere in the middle of the line, rather comfortably (though not without strength and joy) watching others in action. Each function has its blessings and challenges... and I guess part of the fun is trading and sharing positions, all the while realizing that none of this would be possible if we weren't connected to each other."

Color and the Rainbow Connection

The kaleidoscope is an orchestra of color
Whose symphonic patterns of unstruck music
Inspire the mind and tune the heart.
It is the rainbow's voice intoning
      chaotic harmony in continuum.

Color and the Rainbow Connection

Through the ages color has enthralled people. The keener their sensitivity and the higher their consciousness, the deeper their enthrallment with the varying hues of the rainbow.

Ancient man was in awe of the rainbow and was convinced that the secrets of the universe lay hidden within its colors. Modern man, through the invention of the Spectroscope, knows this to be true, for the nature of nearly all matter is revealed through color.

In 1666, Newton produced a rainbow by directing a beam of light through a prism. The prism led to the Spectroscope, which created a better image of the spectrum through the use of lenses.

Invented in 1814 by Joseph von Fraunhofer, the Spectroscope is one of the least known instruments and yet, according to Harold Turner's Antique Scientific Instruments, "In its various forms, the Spectroscope has contributed more to modern science than perhaps any other instrument."

A study of color through the ages reveals that at any given period in history colors played a significant role with respect to superstitions, religions, philosophies, traditions, and even the daily activities of people.

It is said that only in more recent times did the aesthetic and sensuous pleasures of color come into play, and it was then that color was relegated to a more or less taken-for-granted status. Fortunately there is a serious reappraisal of the significance and influence of color underway. Color is in! There are books on color harmony, color psychology, color therapy, color healing, and even books on how to color yourself beautiful.

The significance of the prismatic spectrum is found in everything in life — from angels to zoetrobes. All creation is a technicolor panorama projected on life's large space screen. And each element of the universe vibrates to its own corresponding color, as everything in the world works in harmony with the chromatic color scale.

The full spectrum of color has never been perceived as brilliantly as seen through the inner eye of a blind woman:

> *I understand how scarlet can differ from crimson because I know that the smell of an orange is not the smell of a grapefruit. I can also conceive that colors have shades and guess what shades are. In smell and taste there are varieties not broad enough to be fundamental; so I call them shades . . . The force of association drives me to say that white is exalted and pure, green is exuberant, red suggests love or shame or strength. Without the color or its equivalent, life to me would be dark, barren, a vast blackness.*

> *Thus through an inner law of completeness my thoughts are not permitted to remain colorless. It strains my mind to separate color and sound from objects. Since my education began I have always had things described to me with their colors and sounds, by one with keen senses and a fine feeling for the significant. Therefore, I habitually think of things as colored and resonant. Habit accounts for part. The soul sense accounts for another part. The brain with its five-sensed construction asserts its right and accounts for the rest. Inclusive of all, the unity of the world demands that color be kept in it whether I have cognizance of it or not. Rather than be shut out, I take part in it by discussing it, happy in the happiness of those near to me who gaze at the lovely hues of the sunset or the rainbow.*
> — Helen Keller

Music

Pablo Casals said, "All music is a rainbow." Many composers have revealed the potency of color through their music — from the jazz era blues to Arthur Bliss' "Color Symphony".

The seven colors of the spectrum are attuned to the seven tones of the musical scale. And as each color runs the gamut of shades, it has its own corresponding note on a higher or lower octave. (Notice that the three primary colors comprise the first major scale.)

Sound/Color Correspondences

DO — Red	SOL — Blue
RE — Orange	LA — Purple
MI — Yellow	TI — Violet
FA — Green	DO — Red (Higher Octave)

Astrology

Every zodiac sign has a particular color transmitted to earth by means of the sun. Each planet in our solar system receives one of the seven rays of color. There is even a philosophy of color in relation to minerals and precious stones, and flowers. Each emotion and organ of the body possesses its own particular color and responds to it in a specific way. (The following are correspondences of astrological signs and colors as interpreted by psychic counselor Tony Grosso. The sketches are by Jan Haber.)

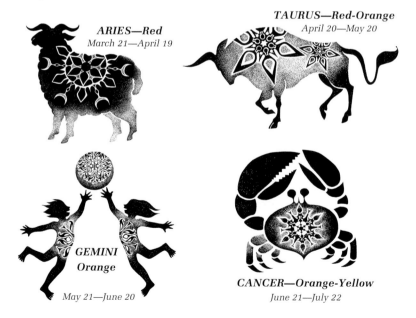

ARIES—Red
March 21—April 19

TAURUS—Red-Orange
April 20—May 20

GEMINI
Orange
May 21—June 20

CANCER—Orange-Yellow
June 21—July 22

LEO—Yellow
July 23— Aug 22

VIRGO
Yellow-Green

Aug 23—Sept 22

LIBRA   **Green**
Sept 23   *Oct 22*

SCORPIO—Green-Blue
Oct 23—Nov 21

SAGITTARIUS—Blue
Nov 22—Dec 21

CAPRICORN—Blue-Violet

Dec 22— Jan 19

AQUARIUS—Violet
Jan 20—Feb 18

PISCES   **Violet-Red**
Feb 19—March 20

169

Healing

The therapeutic and healing value of colors and how they affect our emotional, mental and spiritual body are well recognized. Color is energy. By concentrating on the colors in a kaleidoscope, the proper vibration alignment may be activated in mind and body. Red represents the material realm while violet, at the other end of the spectrum, is the spiritual sphere. Green is the balancing stabilizer between the three stimulating colors (red, orange, and yellow) and the three calming colors (blue, indigo, and violet).

Carol (Toba) Spilman, an artist and exercise teacher working with the healing properties of color, says, "The gift of vision would have little meaning without the gift of color." To increase one's ability to see colors more vividly, Carol suggests an exercise from the ancient Indian holistic healing tradition of Ayurveda (knowledge of life). This simple exercise stimulates the rods and cones of the retina:

Close both eyes and look toward the sun for 15 seconds. Keeping the eyes closed, *gently* massage the eyeballs for 15 seconds. With the eyes still closed, become aware of colors and slowly turn away from the sun. Still keeping your eyes closed, turn back to the sun and away several times, holding each color you see as long as possible.

Chakras

According to ancient Eastern tradition, the seven chakras are spiritual centers, vortices of life force. The word Chakra is of Hindu origin and means "wheel of fire." Edgar Cayce, the most documented psychic of the 20th century, relates the chakra colors to the endocrine system.

Location and Colors Associated with Chakras of the Body

1. Red — located at base of spine
2. Orange — spleen area (2" below navel)
3. Yellow — solar plexus
4. Green — heart
5. Blue — throat
6. Indigo — pineal gland (or third eye)
7. Violet — pituitary gland

Meryl Ann Butler, an artist working in the field of color and healing, designed ChakraScopes (in collaboration with Carolyn Bennett) as a kaleidoscopic aid for meditation and color visualization. To the seven Chakra colors she added four higher octave colors: Fuchsia (the color of transformation), pink (love), gold (the masculine) and silver (the feminine).

A set of seven or eleven small scopes, each wrapped with and containing its own individual color, provides a rainbow's spectrum to focus on or "see" with the inner eye.

But while the properties of color may be universal and relate to specific areas and characteristics, the true perception of color remains personal and individual. Each person possesses his own spectral aura and perceives color according to his own experience and understanding.

Sir Winston Churchill, as a painter and student of color, hinted that there might be higher color cycles in the world beyond:

> *I cannot pretend to be impartial about color. I rejoice with the brilliant ones and am genuinely sorry for the poor browns. When I get to heaven, I mean to spend the first million years in painting and so get to the bottom of the subject. But I shall require a still gayer palette than I get here below. I expect orange and vermilion will be the darkest, dullest colors upon it and beyond them there will be a whole range of wonderful new colors which will delight the celestial eye.*

Moments of Splendor

Celestial colors miraculously perpetuated

Intricate balance beyond human ingress

Delicate completeness within each changing pattern

Interlocking dependencies that underlie all life

Rapturous beauty and nostalgic fragrance

      pervade the kaleidoscope

Creating moments of splendor that keep the spirit

      forever young and fulfilled

SHOPS FEATURING SCOPES

It laughs with changing patterns

Painting colors of rainbow hues

It sings arias of visual enchantment

Caressing the eyes with wondrous views

SHOPS FEATURING SCOPES

More and more gift stores, American craft shops, and art galleries are featuring kaleidoscopes.

From the Nestegg in Bar Harbor, Maine, to the Northwest Shop in Canon Beach, Oregon, there are shops which not only sell handcrafted kaleidoscopes, but whose owners love and appreciate them. And that is the secret to a flourishing scope business. In the stores where the sales people are knowledgeable about the artists and enthusiastic about the scopes' distinguishing characteristics, the differentiation in sales is phenomenal.

Eric Sinizer, owner of the **Light Opera Gallery** in San Francisco, did for the early marketing of kaleidoscopes what the article in the Smithsonian Magazine accomplished in the way of interest and enthusiasm. He was the first to carry an inventory truly representative of the emerging new images.

Eric's involvement with kaleidoscopes is a direct outgrowth of his primary interest in glass. He purchased his first scope at a crafts fair and enjoyed watching the transmission of light through it so much that he got another one — and then another. He put the scopes in his shop so he could enjoy them.

To his surprise, Eric discovered there were a great number of people who appreciated and collected kaleidoscopes. He began amassing the largest collection of scopes available, just as he had done with Russian lacquer boxes and fine glass. He was then the first to publish a catalog devoted solely to kaleidoscopes. Its colorful pictures and succinct descriptions have made it a collector's item itself.

Julian Baird, president of **Tree's Place** in Orleans, Massachusetts, says it was Eric Sinizer's encouragement and unselfishly shared information about kaleidoscope designers that made his life richer and "in far more significant ways than monetary terms."

Julian has been interested in mandalic images for a long time. To him, kaleidoscopic patterns "embody both the static and the dynamic, both earthly and eternal, both still-point and turning wheel of time and space."

As a kaleidoscope mecca, **Hand of the Craftsman** in Nyack, New York proved so successful that it was necessary to open a second store to house more scopes. The Habers' early involvement with kaleidoscopes is a delightful story.

Shel and Jan met as young undergraduates in art school. Romance blossomed, and upon deciding to "go steady," they exchanged gifts. Shel gave Jan an optical prism that scattered rainbows everywhere and she gave him a kaleidoscope. Thirty years later, they are still exchanging optical toys.

Sharing their scopes and encouraging visitors to play have become a way of life at both **Hand of the Craftsman** and **Hand of the Craftsman 2**, just a few short blocks away. Jan explains, "Kaleidoscopes are practically a definition of our gallery's philosophy: that the creative arts, which feed the soul, are also great fun. We have always made a special effort to obtain playful objects for our shop, things that are beautifully crafted and a joy to the hand and the eye as well as an amusing experience."

Art and Donna Milstein are recognized as outstanding leaders in promoting American fine crafts. In their two Houston, Texas locations, **Hanson Galleries** represent this growing movement with the very best in ceramics, wood, hand-blown glass, and a by-product of mixed media — kaleidoscopes!

In September, 1986, Alda Siegan opened the first shop in the country to specialize exclusively in kaleidoscopes and scope-related art. She sold **Kaleido** to Jeannine Wainrib in 1992 after two expansions. Located in Los Angeles, **Kaleido** represents more than 90 artists and displays close to 300 different scopes at all times.

Even though today's kaleidoscopes are being designed for grown-ups more than for children, there are still a few quality toy stores that feature a good variety of scopes.

At **Only Kids** in Memphis, Tennessee, Kathy Arnold stocks scopes that are not just for kids only. In addition to Al Brickel's half-size model of the largest in the world, kids can see a wide variety of scopes their parents would enjoy, and might even catch a showing of Barbara Mitchell's SpectraSphere. This specialized department store for children also features frequent demonstrations and workshops by leading scope artists.

The Red Balloon in Washington, D.C. and **Stardust by the Red Balloon** in McLean, Virginia are two toy stores for children of all ages. Linda Joy and David Meelheim believe that anything to make customers laugh or gasp with delight is fair game for their stores. Kaleidoscopes fit this buying philosophy and then some.

David is fast accomplishing the goal he set for Stardust of having the most complete inventory of kaleidoscopes in the world! Here he carries the major works of over 100 designers and maintains a continuing display of 500 or more scopes.

Karl Schilling at **The Glass Scope** in Red Wing, Minnesota, is one shop owner whose enthusiasm for kaleidoscopes has extended to making them. He conducts frequent workshops to teach his customers how to make their own. Karl also combines his glass working ability to make a few special models to supplement his broad-based inventory. In a glass sculpture "Introspection I," Karl relates life to the visions of beauty and introspection within a kaleidoscope. The symbolism is executed in a clear frosted sandcast sculpture of a standing figure with a chiseled limestone base. A copper end-turning scope projects through the area of the heart.

In addition to selling kaleidoscopes, Mary Wills, co-owner of **Nellie Bly** in Jerome, Arizona, likes to see them utilized as interior decorating objects. "After all," she observes, "kaleidoscopes complement every decorative motif for either the traditional or the contemporary home or office. They are equally appropriate for the living room, dining room, bedroom, kitchen, library, and even the bathroom. To prove the latter point, Mary keeps

(countued on page 185)

Showroom at Stardust by the Red Balloon

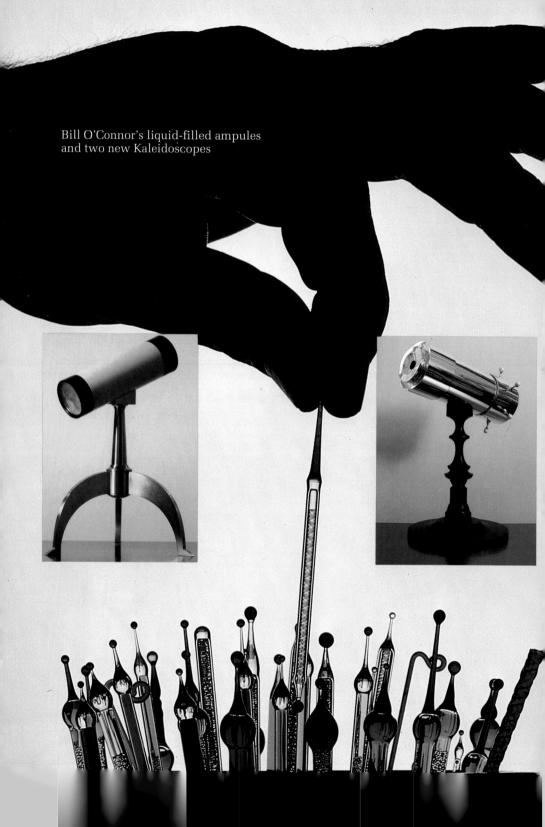

Bill O'Connor's liquid-filled ampules
and two new Kaleidoscopes

Detail of Kaimana Art
Glass scope by
Shantidevi and Ritama

"Kaleiope" by Glenn and Ben Straub   *"Northern Lights" by Amy Hnatko*

Front: Christie Moody, Craig Hopkins   *Rear: Axel Nilsson, Ann and Pete Roberts*

"Silk Dancer"
by **Willie Stevenson**

Adam Peiperl

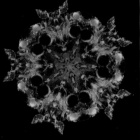

Randy & Shelley Knapp

Mark Reynolds

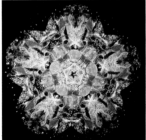

Randy & Shelley Knapp

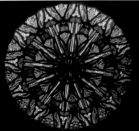

Allen & Michele Crandell

Color-pencil drawing by Betty Tribe

"Dichro-Sphere" by Robert Stephan

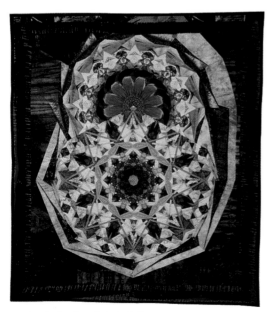

Quilt by Paula Nadelstern
"Turning Point"

Inner-light sculpture by Ray Howlett

182

A fire engine is one of the many objects Joe Polevoi photographs through a C. Bennett Scopelens to achieve a diversity of unique images.

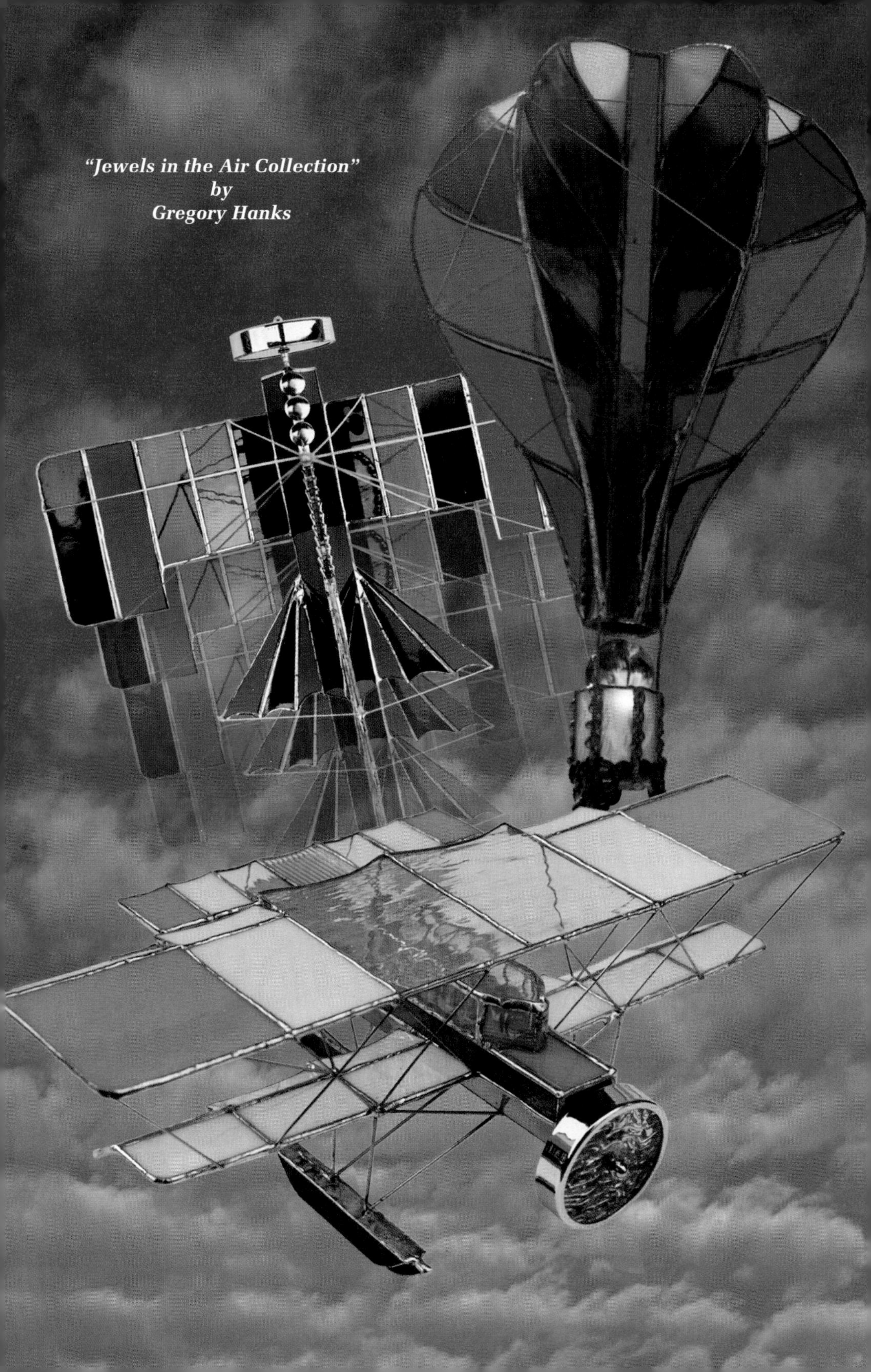

"Jewels in the Air Collection"
by
Gregory Hanks

over 100 kaleidoscopes displayed in her own bathroom.

In addition to highlighting kaleidoscopes in day-to-day sales, several shops and galleries present annual kaleidoscope shows. The **Kentucky Center for the Arts** was the first to spearhead such an annual event shortly after Strathmore's first exhibition. Others soon followed: **Eileen Kremen's Gallery** in Fullerton, California, **The Glass Growers Gallery** in Erie, Pennsylvania, and **Mykonos** in Chadds Ford, Pennsylvania, each of which continues to concentrate on some special aspect of kaleidoscope art each year. Besides an annual exhibition, Tim Beyer, the kaleidoscope buyer for **Davlins** in Minnesota, is so devoted to kaleidoscopes that he has started his own newsletter to keep their customers scope-current and cognizant.

One of the most unexpected shops featuring a full line of kaleidoscopes can be found at a bed and breakfast inn in a small town near Atlanta. At **The Veranda** in Senoia, Georgia, in addition to an impressive selection of kaleidoscopes, there is a 1930 Wurlitzer player piano/organ to accompany scope-viewing, and the evening turn-down treat adorning each fluffy pillow is a tiny kaleidoscope.

Jan and Bobby Boal are the gracious proprietors of this charming Victorian inn and they personally cater to your every whim and appetite, offering not just a continental breakfast, but three delicious home-cooked epicurean meals, plus a gourmet bedtime snack. It's hard to say which is the most appetizing — the food or the scopes, but the combination is unbeatable.

While there is no shop at the **Kaleidoscope Inn** Bed and Breakfast in Baldwin, Wisconsin, it is worth traveling almost any distance to spend a night or two just to see such a fabulous collection of kaleidoscopes.

Located 35 miles east of Minneapolis, Minnesota, Baldwin is a quaint little Dutch community with flower-lined streets and an authentic Dutch windmill.

Clint Anderson is a veterinarian who loves to collect rare and unusual art objects. In 1989 he purchased the Victorian mansion next door to his home and refurbished it with massive, intricately carved furnishings and ornate crystal and stained glass light fixtures, along with a part of his kaleidoscope collection. This makes an ideal setting in which to enjoy the luxury of scope-viewing while listening to an antique nickelodeon.

A few of the outstanding pieces in the collection representing over 60 artists include Barbara Mitchell's SpectraSphere, Willie Stevenson's Home Planet, Amy Hnatko's Fountain of Light, Ward Robison's Seen in the Wood, and Adam Peiperl's Bengal Light.

The Kaatskill Kaleidoscope

From Woodstock, New York, birthplace of the Aquarian Age, comes word of an upcoming major kaleidoscope attraction. Billed as the world's largest kaleidoscope, it is being constructed in the silo of a renovated Civil War-era barn which is part of Catskill Corners, a country shopping complex.

The Kaatskill Kaleidoscope, featuring an innovative configuration of mirrors and objects, is being designed and coordinated by Charles Karadimos. Located off the New York Throughway, it is a two-hour drive from Manhattan. The opening is scheduled for Labor Day, 1993. **Eye Candy**, the project's retail kaleidoscope gallery, will wrap around the new kaleido-silo.

Kaleidoscopes mean more than a well-stocked inventory to David Wallace, owner of **After the Rain** and **The Enchanted Forest** in New York City. Familiar with the technicalities of the different styles and knowledgeable about the artists, David has strong feelings about the kaleidoscope's aesthetic value:

"The kaleidoscope is unique in that it is functionally unnecessary, yet it inspires a devoted, passionate following, the initiation of which is impossible by words, and is made possible only be experience. At its best, it conjures up a combination of the ever-changing and the always-beautiful; like Platonic forms, it remains as an image for that which is perfect, for it contains all that is imperfect, perfectly, with grace and symmetry. It is a tripartite marriage of science, craft, and art, and thus of the mind, the hand, and the heart — which is as close a description of being civilized as we're likely to come upon.

"I do not claim that kaleidoscopes will save us, or heal the planet, or solve racial injustice...(but) they give shape and voice to our lives — and remind us that in our deepest selves lies the desire for beauty and harmony."

Shops Specializing in Kaleidoscopes

ARIZONA

Nellie Bly
Mary Wills & Diane Geoghegan
Main Street
Jerome 86331
(602) 634-0255

CALIFORNIA

Crystal Kaleidoscope
Louis Swisher
710-C Cedar St.
Santa Cruz 95060
(408) 425-1217

Flowers-Just Because
Tedde Ready
2575 N. First St.
San Jose 95131
(408) 456-2970

Kaleido
Jeannine Wainrib
8840 Beverly Boulevard
Los Angeles 90048
(310) 276-6844

Eileen Kremen Gallery
619 N. Harbor Boulevard
Fullerton 92632
(714) 879-1391

Light Opera Gallery
Eric Sinizer
174 Grant Avenue
San Francisco 94108
(800) 553-4800

Petri's Gallery
Bijan Petri
675 Bridgeway
Sausalito 94965
(415) 332-2225

Sun Country
Ray & Diane Anderson
Ocean & San Carlos
Carmel 93921
(408) 625-5907

DISTRICT OF COLUMBIA

The Red Balloon
Linda Joy & David Meelheim
1073 Wisconsin Avenue
Washington 20007
(202) 965-1200

GEORGIA

The Mole Hole of Atlanta
Linda & Steve Hyslop
Phipps Plaza
3500 Peachtree Rd., N.E.
Atlanta, 30326
(404) 231-4840

The Veranda
Jan & Bobby Boal
252 Seavy Street
Senoia 30276-0177
(404) 599-3905

ILLINOIS

The Artists' Works
Judy Kaponya
32 W. Chicago Ave.
Naperville 60540
(708) 357-3774

Kapp's Kaleidoscope
Barbara Kapp
3823 N. Lincoln Ave.
Chicago 60613
(312) 975-3535

Larsen Scope Salon
Paul T. Larsen
1901 Hillside Lane
Lisle 60532
(708) 420-7119

Pam's Glass Works
Pam & Tony Orlando
247 Robert P. Coffin Rd.
Long Grove 60047
(708) 634-6555

Schilling Studio III
Donna & Charles Schilling
228 South Main
DeSoto House Hotel
Galena 61036
(815) 777-3700

INDIANA

Cozy Station
Joan and Sandy Choate
709 W. Main St.
Madison 47250
(812) 265-5757

IOWA

Nook An' Cranny
Corinne Corkey Nydle
Lindale Mall
Cedar Rapids 52402
(319) 393-8771

KENTUCKY

Kentucky Center for the Arts
Karen Townsend
5 Riverfront Plaza
Louisville 40202
(502) 562-0165

LOUISIANA

La Belle Epoque
Babs Ryan and
Gail & Mickey Gowland
The Jackson Brewery
620 Decatur Street
New Orleans 70130
(504) 522-1650

MAINE

The Nestegg Gallery
Linda Shellenberger and
Henry TenBroeke
12 Mount Desert St.
Bar Harbor 04609
(207) 288-9048

MARYLAND

Easy Street
Marcia and Terry Moore
7 Frances Street
Annapolis 21401
(410) 263-5556

Strathmore Hall Arts Center
Kitty Barclay
10701 Rockville Pike
Rockville 20852
(301) 530-0540

Nearly 100 **Natural Wonders** stores carry scopes.
Check the cities near you.

MASSACHUSETTS

Joie de Vivre
Linda Given
1792 Mass Ave.
Cambridge 02140
(617) 864-8188

Impulse
Sonny Bayer
188 Commercial St.
Provincetown 02657
(508) 487-1154

Trees Place
Julian & Elaine Baird
Rt. 6A at 28
Orleans 02653
(508) 255-1330

Whippoorwill Crafts
Karen & Bob Hohler
126 South Market
Faneuil Hall
Boston 02109
(617) 523-5149

MICHIGAN

Chameleon Galleries Ltd.
Nancy Tilly
370 S. Main St.
Plymouth 48170
(313) 455-0445

MINNESOTA

Davlins
David D. Looney
2028 Burnsville Center
Burnsville 55337
(612) 892-3665

Davlins
2652 Southdale Cener
6601 France Ave. S.
Edina 55435
(612) 926-6838

Davlins
116 Rosedale Center
Roseville 55113
(612) 631-2162 & 378-1036

The Glass 'Scope
Karl Schilling
314 Main Street
Riverfront Centre
Red Wing 55066
(612) 388-2048

MISSOURI

Glass Magic, Inc.
Lill Christoffersen
Engler Block
1335 W. Hwy. 76
Branson 65616
(417) 335-8236

NEVADA

Crystal Kaleidoscope
Louis Swisher
1333 Hwy. 395 S. #100
Gardnerville 89410
(702) 782-5552

NEW JERSEY

Dexterity
Shirley Zafirau
26 Church Street
Montclair 07042
(201) 746-5370

Scherer Gallery
Marty & Tess Scherer
93 School Road West
Marlboro 07746
(908) 536-9465

NEW YORK

After the Rain
David Wallace
149 Mercer St.
New York City 10012
(212) 431-1044

Catskill House
Cru Chase
69 Tinker Street
Woodstock 12498
(914) 679-8819

Eye Candy
Dean Gitter
Rt. 28
Mt. Pleasant 12457
(914) 688-2451

Enchanted Forest
David Wallace
85 Mercer St.
New York City 10012
(212) 925-6677

**The Glass
Menagerie**
Jackie & Dick Pope
37 East Market St.
Corning 14830
(607) 962-6300

Hand of the Craftsman
Jan & Shel Haber
52 S. Broadway
Nyack 10960
(914) 358-6622

Hand of the Craftsman 2
Jan & Shel Haber
5 S. Broadway
Nyack 10960
(914) 358-3366

OHIO

The Land of Make Believe
Bruce & Mary McMicken
134 N. Main St.
Hudson 44236
(216) 650-4438

Stonehenge
Kenneth & Katherine
   Benjamin
808 Langram Rd.
Put-in-Bay 43456
(419) 285-6134

OREGON

The Northwest Shop
Lynn Kerege
164 North Hemlock
Cannon Beach 97110
(503) 436-0402

PENNSYLVANIA

A Mano
Ana Leyland
128 S. Main Street
New Hope 18938
(215) 862-5122

Glass Growers Gallery
Debbie Vahanian
701 Holland Street
Erie 16501
(814) 453-3758

Mykonos
Barbara Robbins
Glen Eagle Square
Rt. 202 (P.O. Box 355)
Chadds Ford 19317
(215) 558-8000

Wood You Believe
Glenn & Ben Straub
The Artworks at Doneckers
100 North State St. Studio 126
Ephrata 17522
(717) 738-9595

SOUTH CAROLINA

Smith Galleries of Fine Crafts
Wally & Jean Smith
The Village at Wexford Suite J11
Highway 278
Hilton Head Island 29928
1-800-272-3870

TENNESSEE

Only Kids
Kathy & Stephen Arnold
6150 Poplar Avenue
Memphis 38119
(901) 683-1234

TEXAS

Carlyn Galeries
Cindi Ray
12215 Coit Road
Dallas 75251
(214) 702-0824

Creative Arts Gallery
Helen Merren
836 North Star Mall
San Antonio 78216
(210) 342-8659

FreeFlight Gallery
Sandy Smith
Galleria Mall, Suite 2390
13350 Dallas Parkway
Dallas 75240
(214) 701-9566
and
Westend Marketplace
603 Munger, Suite 309
Dallas 75202
(214) 720-9147

Glass Bookworm
Virginia & Paul Fiehler
311 Spring Cypress
Spring 77033
(713) 288-3396

Hanson Galleries
Donna & Art Milstein
Galleria II, Level III
5085 Westheimer, Suite 3825
Houston 77056
(713) 552-1242
and
Town and Country Mall
800 W. Sam Houston Pkwy, N.
Suite E-118
Houston 77024-3922
(713) 984-1242

VIRGINIA

Stardust by the Red Balloon
Linda Joy & David Meelheim
The Galleria at Tysons II
McLean 22102
(800) 272-6731

BIBLIOGRAPHY

Baker, Cozy, *Kaleidorama,* Beechcliff Books, Annapolis, MD, 1990.

Baker, Cozy, *Through the Kaleidoscope . . . And Beyond,* Beechcliff Books, Annapolis, MD, 1987.

Boswell, Thom, *The Kaleidoscope Book, (A Spectrum of Spectacular Scopes to Make),* Sterling/Lark Books, 1992.

Brewster, Sir David, *A Treatise on the Kaleidoscope* (Edinburgh: Archibald Constable & Co., 1819).

Brewster, Sir David, *The Kaleidoscope — Its History, Theory and Construction with its application to the fine and useful arts,* second, enlarged edition (London: John Murray, 1858)

"The Homelife of Sir David Brewster," by his daughter, Mrs. Margaret Gordon, *The Southern Review,* January 1874, v. 14, No. 29, pp. 53-80.

"Martyr of Science" — Sir David Brewster 1781-1868, Royal Scottish Museum Studios, Edinburgh, Scotland, 1984.

McConnell, Anita, "R. B. Bate of the Poultry: The Life and Times of a Scientific Instrument Maker," Scientific Monograph number 1, London, 1993.

Newlin, Gary and Ledell Murphy, *Cheap Thrills (12 exciting low-cost kaleidoscope projects),* Asheville, NC, 1992.

Smith, Graham, *Disciples of Light, Photographs in the Brewster Album,* The J. Paul Getty Museum, 1990.

Van Cort Publications, Inc., Reprint from Brewster's nineteenth century originals, Holyoke, MA, 1987.

Yoder, Walter D., *Kaleidoscopes, The Art of Mirrored Magic,* (an overview of the historical development, patent literature design techniques and marketing of kaleidoscopes), Albuquerque, NM: By the author, 8417 Capulin NE, 1988.

Kaleido-Glossary

Ampule — Small, sealed glass container.

Annealing — A process that toughens glass.

Birefringent — Doubly refracting material used in polarized-light scopes.

Cell — Same as object case.

Dichroic — Glass showing different colors depending on the angle of light falling on it.

Disc — Object case.

Dihedral — Two-mirror.

First-surface mirror — Reflecting metal is on the front surface of the glass, rather than behind the rear surface as in a conventional mirror.

Flamework — Glass made by using a small flame.

Flashed glass — One color of glass layered onto another color.

Front-surface mirror — Same as first-surface mirror.

Fused glass — Colored pieces of glass laid together and heated until melded.

Hot glass — Scrap glass that has been heated, fused, and painted.

Kaleidoscope — A tubelike instrument containing loose bits and pieces that are reflected by mirrors so that various symmetrical patterns appear as the instrument is rotated. The word kaleidoscope is derived from three Greek words meaning beautiful-form-to see. A basic kaleidoscope consists of an eyepiece, an object case or objects to be viewed, and a set of two, three or more mirrors along its length, angled toward each other. The angle of the mirrors determines the number and complexity of the patterns. The pattern changes when the scope or object case is rotated.

Latticinio — Embedded threads of swirling white and
colored glass.

L.E.D. — Light-emitting diode.

Lens — A piece of glass or other transparent substance
with two opposing curved surfaces, or one plane
surface and one curved surface.

Mandala — A circular design containing concentric geometric
forms, symbolizing the universe, totality, or
wholeness in Hinduism and Buddhism.

Millefiori — Many-cross-section slices of multi-colored
glass in floral-like designs.

Object case — Container at end of scope holding objects
to be viewed.

Oil-suspension — Bits and pieces floating in an oil-filled
object case.

Optically treated mirror — Chemically coated to prevent
discoloration.

Polarized light — Light that vibrates in one plane only
(in contrast to ordinary light, which vibrates
in all directions).

Shards — Slivers of glass.

Slumped glass — Flat glass placed over a mold and heated
until it takes a bent shape.

Teleidoscope — (from the Greek, distant, form, viewing).
A kaleidoscope in which the object case is a lens, or
one having no object case at all. Whatever it is pointed
towards is reflected again and again in kaleidoscopic
patterns.

Videndum (pl. videnda) — From the Latin "that which should
be viewed." Suggested by Dr. Ethan Allen as an
appropriate term for object to be viewed.

THE *B*REWSTER *S*OCIETY

100 Severn Ave., Suite 605
Annapolis, MD 21043
301-365-1855

A Living Kaleidoscope

You are cordially invited to join
The Brewster Society
an association for designers, collectors,
and lovers of kaleidoscopes.

*I*ts purpose is twofold:

A quarterly newsletter keeps you up to date on who's who
and what's what in the world of kaleidoscopes and where to
attend exhibitions, shows, and regional Brewster meetings.

An Annual Convention is for meeting new artists and fellow
enthusiasts, sharing ideas, learning, and viewing new kaleidoscopes.

Annual membership dues — $35.
Canada and foreign — $45 (Postal or International Money
Order, U.S. dollars only.)

_____

Name   (Please Print)

_____

Address

_____

_____

Phone Number

ABOUT THE AUTHOR

When I was a little girl, fireworks and surprise parties were my very favorite things in the whole world. As I grew up, I became fascinated with rainbows and stained glass windows. Then, as I matured, each day's sunrise and sunset kept me enthralled. Now I have captured all my lifetime favorites in one mirrored tube of magic—the kaleidoscope!

It was after the tragic loss of her beloved son Randall, in 1981, that Cozy Baker discovered and turned her attention to the fascinating world of kaleidoscopes. She has since acquired one of the premier collections, written the first book on the subject, and curated the nation's first kaleidoscope exhibition.

After establishing a unique communication networking between kaleidoscope artists, collectors, and shop owners, Cozy founded the Brewster Society, an international organization for scope enthusiasts. She is editor and publisher of its quarterly newsletter and director of an annual convention.

Other books by Cozy Baker are, *A Cozy Getaway, Holiday Frame of Mind, Love Beyond Life, Through the Kaleidoscope,* and *Kaleidorama.*